All-Star 1

Linda Lee

Stephen Sloan ★ **Grace Tanaka** ★ **Shirley Velasco**

 McGraw-Hill

All-Star 1 First Edition

ISBN-13: 978-0-07-284664-5
ISBN-10: 0-07-284664-X (Student Book)
11 QWD/QWD 0 9

ISBN-13: 978-0-07-331935-3
ISBN-10: 0-07-331935-X (Student Book with Audio Highlights)
10 QWD/QWD 0 9

Editorial director Tina B. Carver
Executive editor Erik Gundersen
Director of sales and marketing Thomas P. Dare
Developmental editors Jennifer Monaghan, Mari Vargo
Editorial assistant David Averbach
Production manager Juanita Thompson
Interior designer Wee Design Group
Cover designer Wee Design Group
Illustrators Gioia Fiommenghi, Andrew Lange, Chris Pappas, Carlos Sanchis/NETS, Blanche Sims, Susan Tait-Porcaro, Chris Winn, David Winter, and Jerry Zimmerman
Photo Research NETS
Photo Credits

14 *(left to right, row one)* © Getty Images, © Jonathan Nourok/PhotoEdit, © Dana White/PhotoEdit; (row two) © Michael Newman/PhotoEdit, © Phil Martin/PhotoEdit, © Spencer Grant/PhotoEdit; *(row three)* © Tom Prettyman/PhotoEdit, © Billy E. Barnes/PhotoEdit, © David Young-Wolff/PhotoEdit
30 © Bill Aron/PhotoEdit
31 *(left to right)* © Michelle D. Bridwell/PhotoEdit, © Dennis MacDonald/PhotoEdit
58 *(top to bottom)* © Jeff Greenberg/PhotoEdit, © Mark Richards/PhotoEdit
59 *(clockwise from upper left)* © Bill Aron/PhotoEdit, © Getty Images, © Getty Images, © A. Ramey/PhotoEdit
78 *(left to right, all)* © Getty Images
79 *(table, left to right, row 1, all)* © Getty Images; *(row 2, all)* © Getty Images; *(bottom, left to right)* © Getty Images, © David Young-Wolff/PhotoEdit, © Getty Images
106 © Getty Images
107 *(clockwise from top left)* © Lina Sokolson, © Getty Images, © Spencer Grant/PhotoEdit
110 *(top right)* © Getty Images; *(table, row 1, left to right)* © Cleve Bryant/PhotoEdit, © Getty Images, © Getty Images, © Getty Images *(row 2)* © David Young-Wolff/PhotoEdit, © Getty Images, Getty Images, © Getty Images; *(row three)* © Lon C. Diehl/PhotoEdit, © Bill Aron/PhotoEdit, © Stephen McBrady/PhotoEdit
126 *(top left)* © Tony Freeman; *(top right)* © Michael Newman/PhotoEdit; *(bottom left)* © Michael Newman/PhotoEdit; *(bottom right)* © Spencer Grant/PhotoEdit
139 *(left to right)* © Patrick O'Lear/PhotoEdit, © Jeff Greenberg/PhotoEdit, © Jeff Greenberg/PhotoEdit
142 © Getty Images
145 © Getty Images
158 © Getty Images

ACKNOWLEDGEMENTS

The authors and publisher would like to thank the following individuals who reviewed the *All-Star* program at various stages of development and whose comments, reviews, and field-testing were instrumental in helping us shape the series:

Carol Antunano • The English Center; Miami, FL

Feliciano Atienza • YMCA Elesair Project; New York, NY

Nancy Baxer • Lutheran Social Ministries of New Jersey Refugee Resettlement Program; Trenton, NJ

Jeffrey P. Bright • Albany Park Community Center; Chicago, IL

Enzo Caserta • Miami Palmetto Adult Education Center; Miami, FL

Allison Freiman • YMCA Elesair Project; New York, NY

Susan Gaer • Santa Ana College School of Continuing Education; Santa Ana, CA

Toni Galaviz • Reseda Community Adult School; Reseda, CA

Maria Hegarty • SCALE; Somerville, MA

Virginia Hernandez • Miami Palmetto Adult Education Center; Miami, FL

Giang Hoang • Evans Community Adult School; Los Angeles, CA

Edwina Hoffman • Miami-Dade County Adult Schools; Miami, FL

Ionela Istrate • YMCA of Greater Boston International Learning Center; Boston, MA

Janice Jensen • Santa Ana College School of Continuing Education; Santa Ana, CA

Jan Jerrell • San Diego Community College District; San Diego, CA

Margaret Kirkpatrick • Berkeley Adult School; Berkeley, CA

LaRanda Marr • Oakland Unified School District; Office of Adult Education; Oakland, CA

Patricia Mooney-Gonzalez • New York State Department of Education; Albany, NY

Paula Orias • Piper Community School; Broward County Public Schools; Sunrise, FL

Linda O'Roke • City College of San Francisco; San Francisco, CA

Betsy Parrish • Hamline University; St. Paul, MN

Mary Pierce • Xavier Adult School; New York, NY

Marta Pitt • Lindsey Hopkins Technical Education Center; Miami, FL

Donna Price-Machado • San Diego Community College District; San Diego, CA

Sylvia Ramirez • Community Learning Center • MiraCosta College; Oceanside, CA

Inna Reydel • YMCA of Greater Boston International Learning Center; Boston, MA

Kristin Sherman • Adult ESL Program; Central Piedmont Community College; Charlotte, NC

Leslie Shimazaki • San Diego Community College District; San Diego, CA

Betty Stone • SCALE; Somerville, MA

Theresa Suslov • SCALE; Somerville, MA

Dave VanLew • Simi Valley Adult & Career Institute; Simi Valley, CA

Scope and Sequence

UNIT	Life Skills				
	Listening and Speaking	**Reading and Writing**	**Critical Thinking**	**Vocabulary**	**Grammar**
Pre-Unit **Meeting Your Classmates** *page 2*	• Listen to introductions • Introduce yourself • Ask for and give spelling of names	• Make a name tag		• Personal information (first name, last name) • Alphabet	
1 **Getting Started** *page 4*	• Exchange personal information • Talk about things in a classroom • Follow classroom instructions • Say and understand numbers (telephone, area code, zip code) • Use appropriate greetings and partings • Ask about occupations • Introduce people **Pronunciation Focus:** Long vowel sounds: *I* and *E*	• Read a world map • Read and write classroom instructions • Read for specific information • Read job ads • Read and complete application forms • Make flashcards	• Classify information • Apply what you know • Interpret information (on an application form) • Interpret a world map	• Classroom vocabulary • Countries • Personal information (name, address, etc.) • Occupations	• Personal pronouns • Imperatives • Punctuation **Spotlight:** Simple present of *be*; possessives
2 **Places** *page 20*	• Describe the location of things in the community • Talk about places on a U.S. map • Ask for clarification • Talk about library services **Pronunciation Focus:** Voiced and voiceless *Th* sounds	• Use a telephone directory • Read a map • Read traffic signs • Complete an application for a library card • Write addresses and phone numbers **Spotlight:** Personal interest stories	• Interpret a map • Classify places (public/private) • Interpret an illustration • Interpret traffic signs	• Geographical directions (N, S, E, W) • Places in the community • People and things in a library • Street signs	• Prepositions of location • *There is/There are* • *Is there/Are there* • Singular and plural nouns • Punctuation
3 **Time and Money** *page 36*	• Ask for and tell the time of day • Ask about business hours • Ask about prices • Ask for a phone number from directory assistance • Listen to an automated phone message **Pronunciation Focus:** Syllable stress in numbers	• Read amounts of money • Read and write personal checks • Read a time schedule • Read signs (in the library) • Write time schedules • Describe a scene • Write amounts of money in words and numbers	• Draw conclusions • Classify information • Compare	• Times of day • Time words • Days of the week • Money: coins and bills • Parts of a personal check	• Yes/no questions with *be* • Questions with *how much* **Spotlight:** Yes/No questions and answers with *be*; information questions with *be*

Correlations to National Standards

Civics Concepts	Math Skills	CASAS Life Skill Competencies	SCANS Competencies (Workplace)	EFF Content Standards	Literacy Completion Points (LCPs)
		• 0.1.4, 0.1.6, 0.2.1	• Sociability	• Communicate so that others understand	• 22.02
• Identify countries on a map • Recognize different occupations in the community	• Use numbers 0 to 11 • Understand page references • Read and write telephone numbers and addresses	• **1:** 0.1.2, 0.2.1, 1.1.3, 2.7.2, 6.6.5 • **2:** 0.1.5, 2.2.1, 6.6.5, 7.1.4, 7.4.1 • **3:** 0.1.5, 6.0.2, 7.1.3 • **4:** 0.2.2 • **5:** 0.1.4, 0.1.1 • **6:** 4.1.3, 4.1.8, 4.6.3 • **7:** 0.1.2, 7.1.4, 7.4.7, 7.4.8 • **GS:** 0.1.6	Emphasized are the following: • Know how to learn • See things in the mind's eye • Sociability • Work well with others • Work with people of diverse backgrounds	Emphasized are the following: • Communicate so that others understand • Listen to and learn from others' experiences and ideas	• **1:** 30.02, 32.07, 33.09 • **2:** 33.02 • **3:** 25.01, 32.07 • **4:** 22.01, 32.04, 33.07 • **5:** 22.02, 22.03, 33.02 • **6:** 18.01 • **7:** 32.13 • **GS:** 22.01, 32.02, 33.03
• Identify public services • Locate cities and states in the U.S. • Make a neighborhood map • Identify places in the community • Understand traffic signs • Visit a public library • Complete a library card application	• Understand phone numbers • Read math symbols • Understand spatial relationships	• **1:** 0.1.2, 2.1.1, 2.2.5, 6.7.3 • **2:** 0.1.2, 0.1.6, 1.1.3, 1.9.4 • **3:** 0.1.2, 2.2.1, 2.2.3 • **4:** 1.9.4, 2.2.2, 5.2.4, 6.0.3, 6.0.4 • **5:** 0.1.2, 0.1.6, 2.5.4, 2.6.1 • **6:** 0.1.2, 2.5.5, 2.5.6 • **7:** 0.1.2, 7.1.4, 7.4.7, 7.4.8 • **WS:** 0.2.4, 4.6.1, 7.5.1	Emphasized are the following: • See things in the mind's eye • Understand how systems work	Emphasized are the following: • Get involved in the community and get others involved • Assist others • Find and use community resources and services	• **1:** 29.01 • **2:** 29.01, 32.01, 32.10 • **3:** 26.04, 32.02 • **4:** 26.03, 32.01, 32.06 • **5:** 26.03, 32.01, 32.02 • **6:** 29.01 • **7:** 32.08, 32.13 • **WS:** 32.10, 33.01
• Identify the business hours of places in the community • Distinguish U.S. coins and bills	• Interpret clock time • Use numbers 12 to 90 • Write the time using numbers • Count coins and bills • Read and understand price tags • Write dollar amounts on personal checks • Use addition and subtraction to calculate total costs	• **1:** 0.1.2, 2.3.1, 6.0.2 • **2:** 0.1.2, 0.1.6, 2.3.2, 2.5.4 • **3:** 1.1.2, 1.1.6, 6.0.1 • **4:** 1.8.2, 6.1.1, 6.5.1, 7.3.2 • **5:** 0.1.3, 0.1.4, 2.1.8 • **6:** 1.2.1, 1.2.2, 2.1.1 • **7:** 0.1.2, 7.1.4, 7.4.7, 7.4.8 • **GS:** 7.2.3	Emphasized are the following: • Understand how systems work	Emphasized are the following: • Manage time and resources • Learn new skills	• **1:** 25.01, 25.02 • **2:** 25.03 • **3:** 25.05 • **4:** 32.08 • **5:** 23.02, 25.04 • **6:** 32.07 • **7:** 32.13, 34.02 • **GS:** 33.02, 33.06, 33.07

CASAS and LCP standards: Numbers in bold indicate lesson numbers.   •   **GS:** Grammar Spotlight   •   **WS:** Writing Spotlight

Scope and Sequence

	Life Skills				
UNIT	Listening and Speaking	Reading and Writing	Critical Thinking	Vocabulary	Grammar
4 **Calendars** *page 52*	• Describe the weather • Talk about events on a calendar • Talk about holidays • Talk about appointments • Make, cancel, and reschedule an appointment **Pronunciation Focus:** Short *A* and long *A*	• Read information on a calendar • Read appointment cards • Read and write about holidays • Write appointments and events on a calendar **Spotlight:** Personal interest stories	• Classify information • Evaluate • Interpret information about appointments • Interpret information about a school calendar	• Months of the year • Weather words • Holidays • Ordinal numbers	• *Wh* questions with *be* • Questions with *how many* • Singular and plural nouns • Capitalization
5 **Clothing** *page 68*	• Ask for information in a store • Ask about sizes and prices • Describe clothing • Listen to a story • Give opinions about clothes • Return something to a store • Talk about appropriate clothing **Pronunciation Focus:** Vowel sounds in *shoes* and *should*	• Add words to a Venn diagram • Describe clothes • Read store signs • Read price tags • Read a store receipt • Write a store receipt • Write a personal check • Read a story • Complete a story chart • Read an office memo	• Make inferences • Classify information • Sequence events • Predict • Summarize	• Clothing names • Colors • Department store people, places, and actions • Sizes • Prices • Descriptive words for clothing	• Present continuous statements • Present continuous questions and answers • Object pronouns **Spotlight:** Present continuous statements; information questions with the present continuous
6 **Food** *page 84*	• Give opinions about foods • Ask for items in a grocery store • Describe food containers • Ask for price information • Listen to a recorded message **Pronunciation Focus:** Intonation in *yes/no* questions	• Write a shopping list • Read store flyers • Read store receipts • Interpret a food pyramid • Read a recipe • Connect sentences with *and* • Write a recipe **Spotlight:** Recipes	• Classify information • Make comparisons • Choose the best alternative • Sequence events	• Food • Descriptive words for food • Grocery store places, things, and actions • Food containers • Food groups	• Questions and answers with *do* and *don't* • Frequency adverbs
7 **Families** *page 100*	• Talk about family members and responsibilities • Talk about personal interests and activities • Make telephone calls • Discuss family expenses • Give opinions about expenses **Pronunciation Focus:** Linking consonant to vowel	• Make a family tree • Write about family responsibilities • Read family portraits and take notes • Write about family	• Classify information • Estimate	• Family members • Household activities • Park activities • Family expenses	• *Yes/No* questions + simple present • Simple present statements • *Don't* and *doesn't* **Spotlight:** Simple present statements; information questions with the simple present

Correlations to National Standards

Civics Concepts	Math Skills	CASAS Life Skill Competencies	SCANS Competencies (Workplace)	EFF Content Standards	Literacy Completion Points (LCPs)
• Identify important holidays in the U.S. • Keep community appointments on a calendar • Interpret a child's school calendar	• Use ordinal numbers • Read and write dates • Convert dates to numeric form • Interpret schedules • Understand appointment times and dates	• **1:** 0.1.2, 2.3.2, 6.0.2, 2.7.1 • **2:** 0.1.4, 0.2.3, 2.6.3, 2.7.3 • **3:** 6.0.1, 7.1.2 • **4:** 0.1.2, 2.7.1, 2.7.2 • **5:** 0.1.4, 2.1.8, 3.1.2 • **6:** 2.3.2, 7.1.1, 7.1.4 • **7:** 0.1.2, 7.1.4, 7.4.7, 7.4.8 • **WS:** 2.7.1, 7.5.1	Emphasized are the following: • Problem solving • Self-management • Acquire and evaluate information • Organize and maintain information	Emphasized are the following: • Manage time and resources • Pass on values, ethics, and cultural heritage • Organize, plan, and prioritize work	• **1:** 25.03, 29.03, 30.01 • **2:** 25.01, 32.01, 32.07 • **3:** 24.03, 25.04, 32.02 • **4:** 32.07, 32.10 • **5:** 24.03, 34.03 • **6:** 31.04 • **7:** 32.04, 32.13 • **WS:** 33.06
• Explore a department store • Interpret price tags and receipts • Recognize different occupations in the community	• Understand prices and sales receipts • Use multiplication and division to calculate totals	• **1:** 1.1.9, 1.3.9, 6.6.5 • **2:** 1.3.1, 1.3.7 • **3:** 1.1.4, 1.2.1, 1.2.2, 1.2.4, 4.4.1, 6.1.3 • **4:** 7.2.7 • **5:** 8.1.2 • **6:** 4.4.1, 8.4.1 • **7:** 0.1.2, 7.1.4, 7.4.7, 7.4.8 • **GS:** 7.4.3	Emphasized are the following: • Creative thinking • Reasoning • See things in the mind's eye • Analyze and communicate information	Emphasized are the following: • Provide for physical needs • Reflect on and reevaluate opinions and ideas	• **1:** 28.02 • **2:** 33.03 • **3:** 28.03, 33.03 • **4:** 22.03 • **5:** 19.01 • **6:** 19.01 • **7:** 32.08, 32.10, 32.13 • **GS:** 33.02
• Understand the food groups • Explore a grocery store • Interpret receipts • Understand healthy eating	• Use U.S. measurements: pounds, ounces, and cups • Compare prices • Budget for food • Calculate serving sizes • Read and write measurements for recipes	• **1:** 1.3.8 • **2:** 0.1.2, 1.3.8 • **3:** 1.1.4, 1.1.7, 1.3.8, 6.5.1 • **4:** 1.2.2, 1.2.4, 1.2.5 • **5:** 1.3.3 • **6:** 3.5.1, 3.5.2, 3.5.9 • **7:** 0.1.2, 7.1.4, 7.4.7, 7.4.8 • **WS:** 1.1.1, 8.2.1	Emphasized are the following: • Decision making • Problem solving • See things in the mind's eye • Self-management • Use resources wisely • Teach others new skills • Acquire and evaluate information	Emphasized are the following: • Find and use community resources and services • Find, interpret, and analyze diverse sources of information • Provide for physical needs • Communicate so that others understand	• **1:** 24.05 • **2:** 32.01 • **3:** 28.01 • **4:** 25.05, 28.03 • **5:** 32.01 • **6:** 32.04, 32.07 • **7:** 32.08, 32.13 • **WS:** 32.07
• Discuss community-related activities	• Take messages that include telephone numbers • Create a household budget • Use addition and multiplication to calculate totals	• **1:** 0.2.1, 6.6.8 • **2:** 8.2.1, 8.2.5, 8.2.6, 8.3.1 • **3:** 0.2.4, 2.7.2 • **4:** 7.5.1 • **5:** 2.1.7, 2.1.8 • **6:** 1.5.1, 7.4.9, 7.5.5, 7.5.7 • **7:** 0.1.2, 7.1.4, 7.4.7, 7.4.8 • **GS:** 7.2.2, 7.2.5, 7.3.3	Emphasized are the following: • Self-management • Integrity and honesty • Use resources wisely • Acquire and evaluate information • Organize and maintain information	Emphasized are the following: • Provide a nurturing home environment • Provide for physical needs • Teach children • Establish rules and expectations for children's behavior	• **1:** 31.01 • **2:** 31.03 • **3:** 34.02 • **4:** 34.03 • **5:** 32.02 • **6:** 32.08 • **7:** 32.02, 32.13 • **GS:** 33.07

CASAS and LCP standards: Numbers in bold indicate lesson numbers. • **GS:** Grammar Spotlight • **WS:** Writing Spotlight

Scope and Sequence

UNIT	Listening and Speaking	Reading and Writing	Critical Thinking	Vocabulary	Grammar
	Life Skills				
8 Health *page 116*	• Talk about health problems • Discuss remedies • Listen to and practice 911 calls **Pronunciation Focus:** Linking vowel to vowel with a *Y* or *W* sound	• Read warning labels • Read opinion paragraphs • Read bar graphs • Indent a paragraph • Write an opinion paragraph • Draw a bar graph **Spotlight:** Opinions	• Classify information • Make inferences • Analyze arguments • Make decisions	• Parts of the body • Health problems • Remedies • Safety warnings	• *Can* for ability • Giving advice with *should* and *shouldn't*
9 House and Home *page 132*	• Describe things in a house • Talk about accidents in the home • Ask for housing information **Pronunciation Focus:** Stress in compound nouns	• Write a comparison of two houses • Read bar graphs • Read classified ads • Write a classified ad • Read bills • Write personal checks	• Compare and contrast • Choose the best alternative • Classify information • Make decisions	• Areas of a house • Household furniture and other items • Features of a house • Types of housing • Classified ad abbreviations • Utility bills	• Comparing past and present • Simple past statements • Negative simple past statements **Spotlight:** Simple past statements; information questions with the simple past
10 Work *page 148*	• Respond to job ads • Listen to a job interview • Give opinions about what to do in an interview • Give reasons **Pronunciation Focus:** Stressing important words in sentences	• Read and write help wanted ads • Read a success story • Write a story • Read for specific information • Complete job applications • Complete an idea list **Spotlight:** Past tense stories	• Classify information • Reason • Sequence events	• Occupations and skills • Help wanted ad abbreviations • Work experience	• *Yes/No* questions with the simple past • Future with *be going to*

Appendices

Correlations to National Standards

Civics Concepts	Math Skills	CASAS Life Skill Competencies	SCANS Competencies (Workplace)	EFF Content Standards	Literacy Completion Points (LCPs)
• Explore a health clinic • Understand safety warnings • Understand when to call 911 • Explore a hospital	• Use U.S. measurements: gallons, quarts, pints, cups and ounces • Interpret bar graphs	• **1**: 3.1.1 • **2**: 3.1.1 • **3**: 3.4.3 • **4**: 3.3.1, 3.4.1, 3.4.2, 6.6.1 • **5**: 2.1.2, 2.5.1 • **6**: 2.2.1, 3.1.3, 2.5.3, 7.4.4 • **7**: 0.1.2, 7.1.4, 7.4.7, 7.4.8 • **WS**: 7.3.4, 7.4.2	Emphasized are the following: • Reasoning • See things in the mind's eye • Integrity and honesty • Organize and maintain information	Emphasized are the following: • Provide for physical needs • Find and use community resources and services • Exercise human and legal rights and civic responsibilities • Help self and others	• **1**: 24.01 • **2**: 32.01 • **3**: 32.10 • **4**: 24.04, 27.02 • **5**: 23.01, 27.01 • **6**: 24.02 • **7**: 32.10, 32.13 • **WS**: 32.05, 32.08
• Recognize different types of housing in a community • Use classified ads as a source of community information	• Interpret bar graphs • Compare rent prices for apartments and houses • Interpret and pay bills	• **1**: 1.4.1 • **2**: 1.4.2 • **3**: 0.1.6, 3.4.2, 6.7.2 • **4**: 1.4.2 • **5**: 2.1.8, 2.2.1, 7.5.5 • **6**: 1.5.1, 1.5.3, 1.8.2, 2.4.1 • **7**: 0.1.2, 7.1.4, 7.4.7, 7.4.8 • **GS**: 0.2.1, 0.2.4	Emphasized are the following: • Decision making • See things in the mind's eye • Acquire and evaluate information	Emphasized are the following: • Find, interpret, and analyze diverse sources of information • Provide for physical needs • Find and use community resources and services	• **1**: 28.04 • **2**: 32.07 • **3**: 32.04 • **4**: 28.04 • **5**: 23.02 • **6**: 25.06, 28.05 • **7**: 32.13 • **GS**: 33.07
• Use help wanted ads as a source of community information • Recognize some dos and don'ts of interviewing	• Solve word problems • Understand hourly wages • Use addition and multiplication to calculate totals	• **1**: 4.1.6, 4.4.2, 6.6.5 • **2**: 4.4.4, 4.4.5, 4.4.6, 4.4.7 • **3**: 4.1.2, 4.1.5, 4.1.7 • **4**: 4.1.9 • **5**: 4.1.2, 4.1.7 • **6**: 4.1.2 • **7**: 0.1.2, 7.1.4, 7.4.7, 7.4.8 • **WS**: 7.5.2, 7.5.4	Emphasized are the following: • Problem solving • Self-esteem • Integrity and honesty • Acquire and evaluate information • Analyze and communicate information • Work within the system	Emphasized are the following: • Find and get a job • Plan and renew career goals • Find, interpret, and analyze diverse sources of information	• **1**: 32.01 • **2**: 18.02 • **3**: 20.02 • **4**: 32.02 • **5**: 18.02, 20.02 • **6**: 18.03 • **7**: 32.08, 32.13 • **WS**: 32.01, 32.10

CASAS and LCP standards: Numbers in bold indicate lesson numbers. • **GS**: Grammar Spotlight • **WS**: Writing Spotlight

All-Star is a four-level, standards-based series for English learners featuring a picture-dictionary approach to vocabulary building. "Big picture" scenes in each unit provide springboards to a wealth of activities developing all of the language skills.

An accessible and predictable sequence of lessons in each unit systematically builds language and math skills around life-skill topics. *All-Star* presents family, work, *and* community topics in each unit, and provides alternate application lessons in its Workbooks, giving teachers the flexibility to customize the series for a variety of student needs and curricular objectives. *All-Star* is tightly correlated to all of the major national and state standards for adult instruction.

Features

★ **Accessible "big picture" scenes** present life-skills vocabulary and provide engaging contexts for all-skills language development.

★ **Predictable sequence of eight, two-page lessons** in each unit reduces prep time for teachers and helps students get comfortable with the pattern of each lesson type.

★ **Flexible structure** allows teachers to customize each unit to meet a variety of student needs and curricular objectives, with application lessons addressing family, work, and community topics in both the Student Book and Workbook.

★ **Comprehensive coverage of key standards, such as CASAS, SCANS, EFF, and LCPs,** prepares students to master a broad range of critical competencies.

★ **Multiple assessment measures** like CASAS-style tests and performance-based assessment offer a broad range of options for monitoring and assessing learner progress.

★ **Dynamic, Interactive CD-ROM program** integrates language, literacy, and numeracy skill building with computer practice.

The Complete *All-Star* Program

★ The **Student Book** features ten, 16-page units, integrating listening, speaking, reading, writing, grammar, math, and pronunciation skills with life-skill topics, critical thinking activities, and civics concepts.

★ The **Student Book with Audio Highlights** provides students with audio recordings of all of the dialogs in the Student Book. This audio CD also includes recordings of all of the new vocabulary presented in the "big picture" scenes.

★ The **Teacher's Edition with Tests** provides:
  • Step-by-step procedural notes for each Student Book activity
  • 250 expansion activities for Student Book 1, many of which offer creative tasks tied to the "big picture" scenes in each unit
  • Culture, Grammar, and Pronunciation Notes
  • Two-page written test for each unit (*Note:* Listening passages for the tests are available on the Student Book Audiocassettes and Audio CDs.)

  • Audio scripts for all audio program materials
  • Answer keys for Student Book, Workbook, and Tests

★ The **Interactive CD-ROM** incorporates and extends the learning goals of the Student Book by integrating language, literacy, and numeracy skill building with multimedia practice on the computer. A flexible set of activities correlated to each unit builds vocabulary, listening, reading, writing, and test-taking skills.

★ The **Color Overhead Transparencies** encourage teachers to present new vocabulary and concepts in fun and meaningful ways. This component provides a full-color overhead transparency for each of the "big picture" scenes.

★ The **Workbook** includes supplementary practice activities correlated to the Student Book. As a bonus feature, the Workbook also includes alternate application lessons addressing the learner's role as worker, family member, and/or community member. These additional, optional lessons may be used in addition to, or as substitutes for, the application lessons found in Lesson 6 of each Student Book unit.

★ The **Audiocassettes** and **Audio CDs** contain recordings for all listening activities in the Student Book. Listening passages for each unit test are provided at the end of the audio section for that unit.

Overview of the *All-Star* Program

UNIT STRUCTURE

Consult the *Welcome to All-Star* guide on pages xiv–xix. This guide offers teachers and administrators a visual tour of one Student Book unit.

All-Star is designed to maximize accessibility and flexibility. Each unit contains the following sequence of eight, two-page lessons that develop vocabulary and build language, grammar, and math skills around life-skill topics:

★ Lesson 1: Vocabulary

★ Lesson 2: Vocabulary in Action

★ Lesson 3: Talk About It

★ Lesson 4: Reading and Writing

★ Lesson 5: Conversation

★ Lesson 6: Application

★ Lesson 7: Review and Assessment

★ Grammar or Writing Spotlight

Each lesson addresses a key adult standard, and these standards are indicated in the upper right-hand corner of each lesson in a yellow bar.

SPECIAL FEATURES OF EACH UNIT

★ *Window on Grammar.* Grammar is presented and practiced in each unit in blue boxes called *Windows on Grammar.* These short presentations offer students small, manageable chunks of grammar that correlate with a variety of national and state standards. *Window on Grammar* boxes provide for written and oral practice of new language structures and functions. Students and teachers will find additional, in-depth grammar practice in a series of two-page lessons called *Spotlight: Grammar* presented throughout the book. A comprehensive *Grammar Reference Guide* at the back of the book summarizes all of the structures and functions presented.

★ *Window on Math.* Learning basic math skills is critically important for success in school, on the job, and at home. As such, national and state standards for adult education mandate instruction in basic math skills. In each unit, a blue box called *Window on Math* is dedicated to helping students develop the functional numeracy skills they need for basic math work.

★ *Window on Pronunciation.* The culminating activity in Lesson 5 (*Conversation*) of each unit is featured in a blue box called *Window on Pronunciation*. This special feature has two major goals: (1) helping students hear and produce specific sounds, words, and minimal pairs of words so they become better listeners and speakers; and (2) addressing issues of stress, rhythm, and intonation so that the students' spoken English becomes more comprehensible.

★ *Spotlight: Grammar and Spotlight: Writing.* At the end of each unit, students and teachers will find either a *Grammar Spotlight* or a *Writing Spotlight*. These are optional, two-page lessons that offer a supplementary focus on grammar or writing skill development.

TWO-PAGE LESSON FORMAT

The lessons in *All-Star* are designed as two-page spreads. Lessons 5–7 and the Spotlights employ a standard textbook layout, but Lessons 1–4 follow an innovative format with a list of activities on the left-hand page of the spread and picture-dictionary visuals supporting these activities on the right-hand page. The list of activities, entitled *Things To Do*, allows students and teachers to take full advantage of the visuals in each lesson, inviting students to achieve a variety of learning goals with them.

"BIG PICTURE" SCENES

Each unit includes one "big picture" scene in either Lesson 2 or Lesson 3. This scene is the visual centerpiece of each unit, and serves as a springboard to a variety of activities provided in the Student Book, Teacher's Edition, Color Overhead Transparencies package, and Interactive CD-ROM program. In the Student Book, the "big picture" scene introduces key vocabulary and serves as a prompt for classroom discussion. The scenes feature characters with distinct personalities for students to enjoy, respond to, and talk about. There are also surprising elements for students to discover in each "big picture" scene.

The Teacher's Edition includes a variety of all-skills "Big Picture Expansion" activities that are tied to the Student Book scenes. For each unit, these expansion activities address listening, speaking, reading, writing, *and* grammar skill development, and allow

teachers to customize their instruction to meet the language learning needs of each group of students.

In the Color Overhead Transparencies package, teachers will find transparencies of each "big picture" scene, which they can use to introduce the vocabulary and life-skill concepts in each unit. They can also use these transparencies to facilitate the "Big Picture Expansion" activities in the Teacher's Edition.

Finally, the Interactive CD-ROM program highlights an additional aspect of the "big picture" scenes in its listening activities. Students working with the CD-ROM program listen to a series of new conversations taking place between characters in the "big picture" scenes. They then work through a series of interactive activities based on these conversations and receive immediate feedback on their work.

CIVICS CONCEPTS

Many institutions focus direct attention on the importance of civics instruction for English language learners. Civics instruction encourages students to become active and informed community members. Throughout each *All-Star* unit, students and teachers will encounter *Try This* activities that introduce students to civics concepts and encourage community involvement. In addition, *Application* lessons provide activities that help students develop their roles as workers, parents, and citizens. Those lessons targeting the students' role as citizen encourage learners to become more active and informed members of their communities.

CASAS, SCANS, EFF, LCPs, AND OTHER STANDARDS

Teachers and administrators benchmark student progress against national and/or state standards for adult instruction. With this in mind, *All-Star* carefully integrates instructional elements from a wide range of standards including CASAS, SCANS, EFF, and the Literacy Completion Points (LCPs). Unit-by-unit correlations of these standards appear in the scope and sequence on pages iv–ix. Here is a brief overview of our approach to meeting the key national and state standards:

★ **CASAS.** Many U.S. states, including California, tie funding for adult education programs to student performance on the Comprehensive Adult Student Assessment System (CASAS). The CASAS (www.casas.org) competencies identify more than 300 essential skills that adults need in order to succeed in the classroom, workplace, and community. Examples of these skills include identifying or using appropriate non-verbal behavior in a variety of settings, responding appropriately to common personal information questions, and comparing price or quality to determine the best buys. *All-Star* comprehensively integrates all of the CASAS Life Skill Competencies throughout the four levels of the series. Level 1 addresses all of the CASAS Level A Life Skills test items on Test Forms 31, 32, 51, and 52.

★ **SCANS.** Developed by the United States Department of Labor, SCANS is an acronym for the Secretary's Commission on Achieving Necessary Skills (wdr.doleta.gov/SCANS/). SCANS competencies are workplace skills that help people compete more effectively in today's global economy. The following are examples of SCANS competencies: works well with others, acquires and evaluates information, and teaches others new skills. A variety of SCANS competencies is threaded throughout the activities in each unit of *All-Star*. The incorporation of these competencies recognizes both the intrinsic importance of teaching workplace skills and the fact that many adult students are already working members of their communities.

★ **EFF.** Equipped for the Future (EFF) is a set of standards for adult literacy and lifelong learning, developed by The National Institute for Literacy (www.nifl.gov). The organizing principle of EFF is that adults assume responsibilities in three major areas of life — as workers, as parents, and as citizens. These three areas of focus are called "role maps" in the EFF documentation. In the parent role map, for example, EFF highlights these and other responsibilities: participating in children's formal education and forming and maintaining supportive family relationships. Each *All-Star* unit addresses all three of the EFF role maps in its *Application* lessons. Lesson 6 in each Student Book unit includes one of the three application lessons for that unit. The remaining two application lessons are found in the corresponding Workbook unit.

★ **LCPs.** Florida and Texas document the advancement of learners in an adult program through their system of Literacy Completion Points (LCPs). *All-Star* Level 1 incorporates into its instruction the vast majority of standards at LCP Level B.

NUMBER OF HOURS OF INSTRUCTION

The *All-Star* program has been designed to accommodate the needs of adult classes with 70–180 hours of classroom instruction. Here are three recommended ways in which various components in the *All-Star* program can be combined to meet student and teacher needs.

★ **70–100 hours.** Teachers are encouraged to work through all of the Student Book materials, incorporating the *Grammar* and *Writing Spotlights* as time permits. The Color Overhead Transparencies can be used to introduce and/or review materials in each unit. Teachers should also look to the Teacher's Edition for teaching suggestions and testing materials as necessary.

Time per unit: 7–10 hours.

★ **100–140 hours.** In addition to working through all of the Student Book materials, teachers are encouraged to incorporate the Workbook and Interactive CD-ROM activities for supplementary practice.

Time per unit: 10–14 hours.

★ **140–180 hours.** Teachers and students working in an intensive instructional setting can take advantage of the wealth of expansion activities threaded through the Teacher's Edition to supplement the Student Book, Workbook, and Interactive CD-ROM materials.

Time per unit: 14–18 hours.

ASSESSMENT

The *All-Star* program offers teachers, students, and administrators the following wealth of resources for monitoring and assessing student progress and achievement:

★ **Standardized testing formats.** *All-Star* is correlated to the CASAS competencies and many other national and state standards for adult learning. Students have the opportunity to practice answering CASAS-style listening and reading questions in Lesson 7 of each unit (*What do you know?*), in Lesson 7 of the Workbook (*Practice Test*), and in the Interactive CD-ROM program. Students practice with the same item types and bubble-in answer sheets they encounter on CASAS and other standardized tests.

★ **Achievement tests.** The *All-Star* Teacher's Edition includes end-of-unit tests. These paper-and-pencil tests help students demonstrate how well they have learned the instructional content of the unit. Adult learners often show incremental increases in learning that are not always measured on the standardized tests. The achievement tests may demonstrate learning even in a short amount of instructional time. Twenty percent of each test includes questions that encourage students to apply more academic skills such as determining meaning from context, making inferences, and understanding main ideas. Practice with these question types will help prepare students who may want to enroll in academic classes.

★ **Performance-based assessment.** *All-Star* provides several ways to measure students' performance on productive tasks, including the *Writing Spotlights* and *Conversation Checks* that have corresponding rubrics in the Student Book to facilitate self-assessment. In addition, the Teacher's Edition suggests writing and speaking prompts that teachers can use for performance-based assessment. These prompts derive from the "big picture" scene in each unit and provide rich visual input as the basis for the speaking and writing tasks asked of the students.

★ **Portfolio assessment.** A portfolio is a collection of student work that can be used to show progress. Examples of work that the instructor or the student may submit in the portfolio include writing samples, speaking rubrics, audiotapes, videotapes, or projects. Every Student Book unit includes several *Try This* activities. These activities require critical thinking and small-group project work. As such, they can be included in a student's portfolio. The Teacher's Edition identifies activities that may be used as documentation for the secondary standards defined by the National Reporting System.

★ **Self-assessment.** Self-assessment is an important part of the overall assessment picture, as it promotes student involvement and commitment to the learning process. When encouraged to assess themselves, students take more control of their learning and are better able to connect the instructional content with their own goals. The Student Book includes *Learning Logs* at the end of each unit, which allow students to check off the vocabulary they have learned and skills they have acquired. The Workbook provides self-check boxes in each lesson, encouraging students to monitor their own progress on individual activities and across units.

★ **Other linguistic and non-linguistic outcomes.** Traditional testing often does not account for the progress made by adult learners with limited educational experience or low literacy levels. Such learners tend to take longer to make smaller language gains, so the gains they make in other areas are often more significant. These gains may be in areas such as self-esteem, goal clarification, learning skills, and access to employment, community involvement and further academic studies. The SCANS and EFF standards identify areas of student growth that are not necessarily language based. *All-Star* is correlated with both SCANS and EFF standards. Every unit in the student book contains a lesson that focuses on one of the EFF role maps (worker, family member, community member), and the Workbook provides alternate lessons that address the other two role maps. Like the Student Book, the Workbook includes activities that may provide documentation that can be added to a student portfolio.

About the author and series consultants

Linda Lee is lead author on the *All-Star* series. Linda has taught ESL/ELT in the United States, Iran, and China, and has authored or co-authored a variety of successful textbook series for English learners. As a classroom instructor, Linda's most satisfying teaching experiences have been with adult ESL students at Roxbury Community College in Boston, Massachusetts.

Stephen Sloan is Title One Coordinator at James Monroe High School in the Los Angeles Unified School District. Steve has more than 25 years of teaching and administrative experience with both high school and adult ESL learners. Steve is also the author of McGraw-Hill's *Rights and Responsibilities: Reading and Communication for Civics.*

Grace Tanaka is professor and coordinator of ESL at the Santa Ana College School of Continuing Education, in Santa Ana, California, which serves more than 20,000 students per year. She is also a textbook co-author and series consultant. Grace has 23 years of teaching experience in both credit and non-credit ESL programs.

Shirley Velasco is assistant principal at Palmetto Adult Education Center in Miami, Florida. She has been a classroom instructor and administrator for the past 24 years. At Palmetto, Shirley has created a large adult ESOL program based on a curriculum she developed to help teachers implement the Florida LCPs (Literacy Completion Points).

Welcome to All-Star

All-Star is a four-level series featuring a "big picture" approach to meeting adult standards that systematically builds language and math skills around life-skill topics.

Predictable unit structure includes the same logical sequence of eight two-page lessons in each unit.

Accessible, two-page lesson format follows an innovative layout with a list of activities labeled "Things To Do" on the left and picture-dictionary visuals on the right.

Comprehensive coverage of key standards such as CASAS, SCANS, EFF, and LCPs prepares students to master critical competencies.

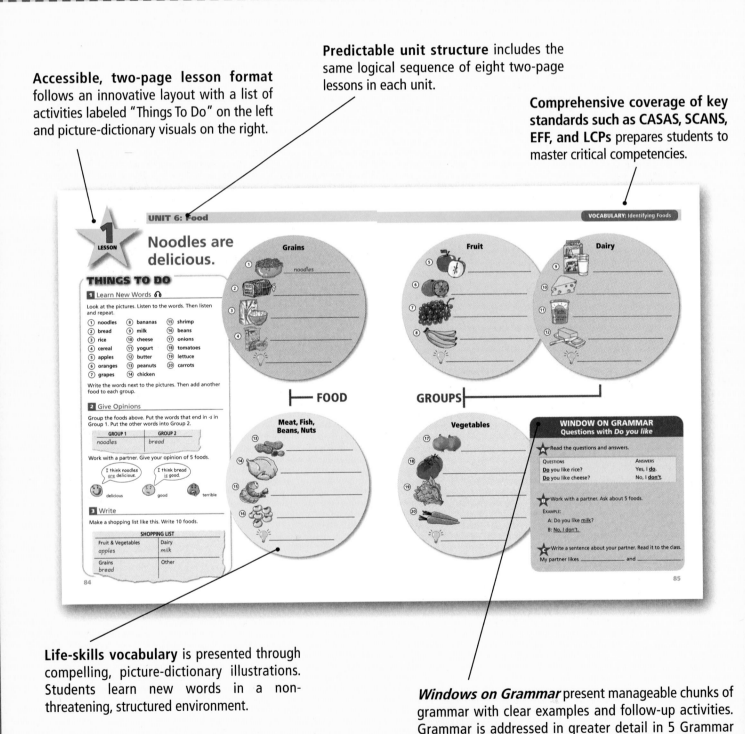

Life-skills vocabulary is presented through compelling, picture-dictionary illustrations. Students learn new words in a non-threatening, structured environment.

Windows on Grammar present manageable chunks of grammar with clear examples and follow-up activities. Grammar is addressed in greater detail in 5 Grammar Spotlights throughout the book and in the Grammar Reference Guide at the back of the book.

"Big picture" scenes are springboards to a wealth of all-skills expansion activities in the Teacher's Edition and Interactive CD-ROM.

Color overhead transparencies for the "big picture" scenes provide fun and meaningful ways to present new vocabulary and concepts.

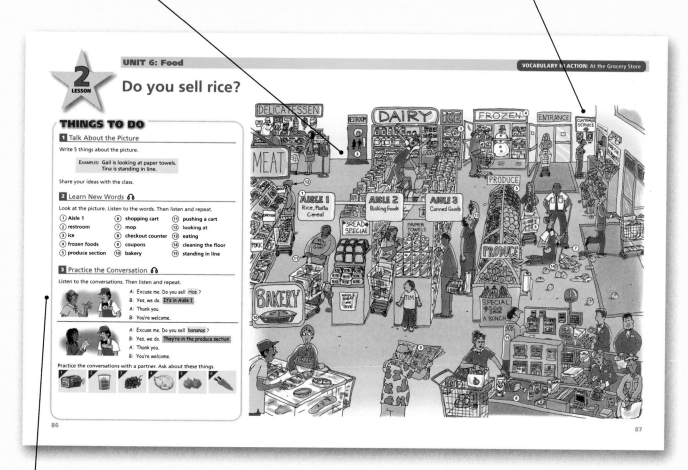

Structured speaking activities invite students to discuss the picture dictionary scene, simulate real-life conversations, and express their thoughts and opinions.

Reading activities develop critical thinking skills by asking students to find important information and make inferences.

Realia-based readings and narrative selections like maps, advertisements, descriptive paragraphs, and short stories provide the basis for developing reading skills.

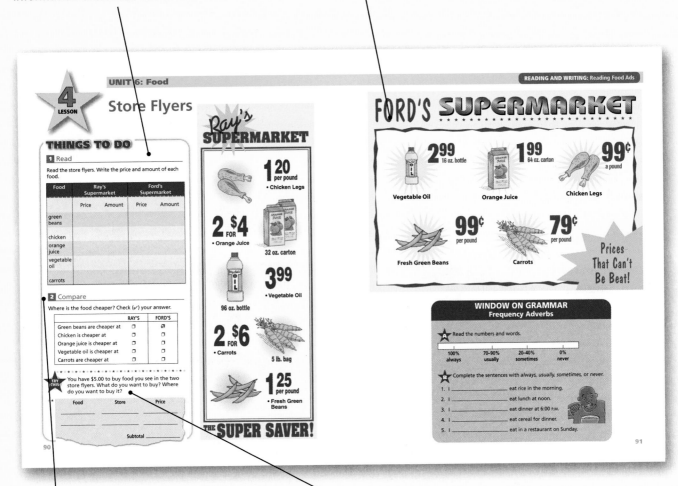

Store Flyers

4 LESSON

READING AND WRITING: Reading Food Ads

THINGS TO DO

1 Read

Read the store flyers. Write the price and amount of each food.

Food	Ray's Supermarket		Ford's Supermarket	
	Price	Amount	Price	Amount
green beans				
chicken				
orange juice				
vegetable oil				
carrots				

2 Compare

Where is the food cheaper? Check (✓) your answer.

	RAY'S	FORD'S
Green beans are cheaper at	☐	☑
Chicken is cheaper at	☐	☐
Orange juice is cheaper at	☐	☐
Vegetable oil is cheaper at	☐	☐
Carrots are cheaper at	☐	☐

TRY THIS You have $5.00 to buy food you see in the two store flyers. What do you want to buy? Where do you want to buy it?

Food	Store	Price
	Subtotal	

Ray's SUPERMARKET

1²⁰ per pound
• Chicken Legs

2 FOR $4
• Orange Juice
32 oz. carton

3⁹⁹
• Vegetable Oil
96 oz. bottle

2 FOR $6
• Carrots
5 lb. bag

1²⁵ per pound
• Fresh Green Beans

THE SUPER SAVER!

FORD'S SUPERMARKET

2⁹⁹ 16 oz. bottle
Vegetable Oil

1⁹⁹ 64 oz. carton
Orange Juice

99¢ a pound
Chicken Legs

99¢ per pound
Fresh Green Beans

79¢ per pound
Carrots

Prices That Can't Be Beat!

WINDOW ON GRAMMAR
Frequency Adverbs

A Read the numbers and words.

100%	70-90%	20-40%	0%
always	usually	sometimes	never

B Complete the sentences with *always, usually, sometimes,* or *never.*

1. I _____ eat rice in the morning.
2. I _____ eat lunch at noon.
3. I _____ eat dinner at 6:00 P.M.
4. I _____ eat cereal for dinner.
5. I _____ eat in a restaurant on Sunday.

90

91

Abundant opportunities for writing prepare students for a variety of academic and real-world writing challenges, such as completing standard forms and writing complete sentences.

Try This activities promote civics concepts by connecting classroom learning to community experiences.

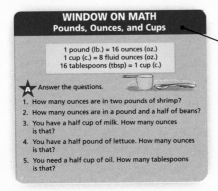

WINDOW ON MATH
Pounds, Ounces, and Cups

1 pound (lb.) = 16 ounces (oz.)
1 cup (c.) = 8 fluid ounces (oz.)
16 tablespoons (tbsp) = 1 cup (c.)

A Answer the questions.

1. How many ounces are in two pounds of shrimp?
2. How many ounces are in a pound and a half of beans?
3. You have a half cup of milk. How many ounces is that?
4. You have a half pound of lettuce. How many ounces is that?
5. You need a half cup of oil. How many tablespoons is that?

Windows on Math help students build numeracy skills for basic math work.

Practice the Conversation activities invite students to engage in everyday conversations with their classmates, using the vocabulary and grammar they have learned.

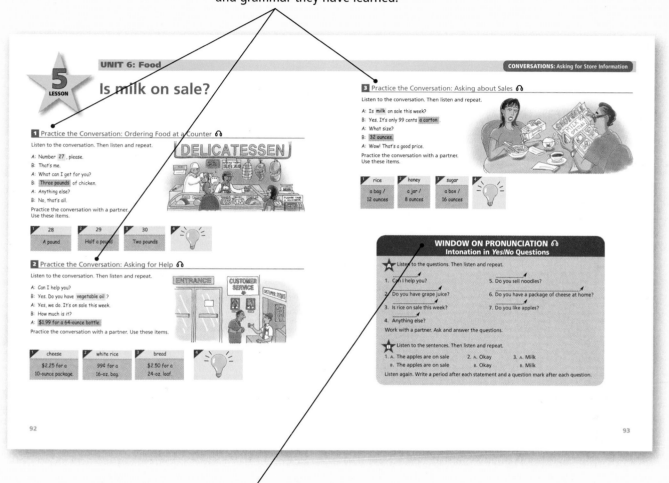

UNIT 6: Food

5 **LESSON**

Is milk on sale?

1 Practice the Conversation: Ordering Food at a Counter 🎧

Listen to the conversation. Then listen and repeat.

A: Number 27 , please.
B: That's me.
A: What can I get for you?
B: Three pounds of chicken.
A: Anything else?
B: No, that's all.

Practice the conversation with a partner. Use these items.

1 28	**2** 29	**3** 30	**4**
A pound	Half a pound	Two pounds	

2 Practice the Conversation: Asking for Help 🎧

Listen to the conversation. Then listen and repeat.

A: Can I help you?
B: Yes. Do you have vegetable oil ?
A: Yes, we do. It's on sale this week.
B: How much is it?
A: $1.99 for a 64-ounce bottle.

Practice the conversation with a partner. Use these items.

1 cheese	**2** white rice	**3** bread	**4**
$2.25 for a 10-ounce package.	99¢ for a 16-oz. bag.	$2.50 for a 24-oz. loaf.	

CONVERSATIONS: Asking for Store Information

3 Practice the Conversation: Asking about Sales 🎧

Listen to the conversation. Then listen and repeat.

A: Is milk on sale this week?
B: Yes. It's only 99 cents a carton .
A: What size?
B: 32 ounces.
A: Wow! That's a good price.

Practice the conversation with a partner. Use these items.

1 rice	**2** honey	**3** sugar	**4**
a bag / 12 ounces	a jar / 8 ounces	a box / 16 ounces	

WINDOW ON PRONUNCIATION 🎧
Intonation in *Yes/No Questions*

⭐ Listen to the questions. Then listen and repeat.

1. Can I help you?
2. Do you have grape juice?
3. Is rice on sale this week?
4. Anything else?
5. Do you sell noodles?
6. Do you have a package of cheese at home?
7. Do you like apples?

Work with a partner. Ask and answer the questions.

⭐ Listen to the sentences. Then listen and repeat.

1. A. The apples are on sale   2. A. Okay   3. A. Milk
   B. The apples are on sale   B. Okay   B. Milk

Listen again. Write a period after each statement and a question mark after each question.

Windows on Pronunciation help students produce difficult sounds in English and address issues of stress, rhythm, and intonation.

Interactive CD-ROM program incorporates and extends the learning goals of each Student Book unit by integrating language, literacy, and numeracy skill building with computer practice.

All-Star
Interactive CD-ROM
LEVEL ⭐

Linda Lee ★ Jean Bernard ★ Stephen Sloan
Grace Tanaka ★ Shirley Velasco

SYSTEM REQUIREMENTS:
Information goes here. Information goes here. Information goes here. Information goes here. Information goes here.

Application lessons focus on developing the students' roles in life as workers, parents, and citizens.

Real-world documents and situations are highlighted in the *Application* lessons, exposing students to critical concepts they encounter at work, at home, and in the community.

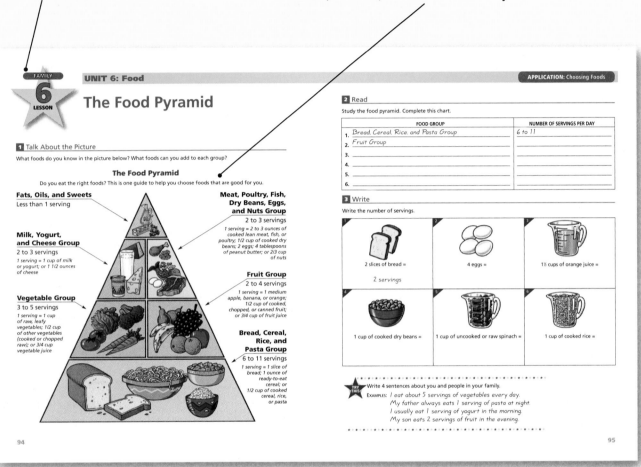

Alternate application lessons in the Workbook provide a flexible approach to addressing family, work, *and* community topics in each unit.

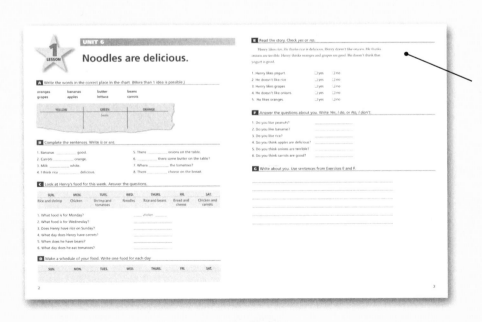

Listening Reviews help teachers assess listening comprehension, while giving students practice with the item types and answer sheets they encounter on standardized tests.

Conversation Checks are communicative information gap activities that also provide informal listening and speaking self-assessment tools.

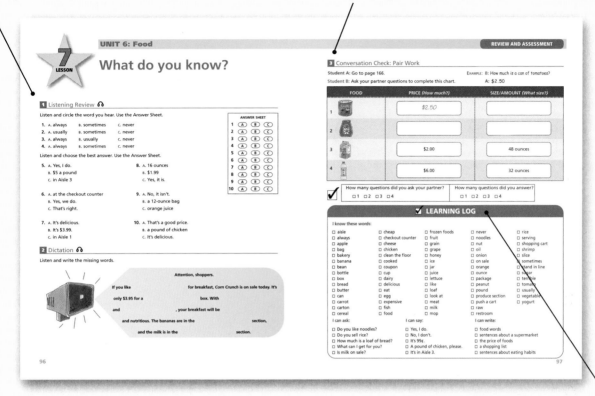

A **Grammar** or **Writing Spotlight** appears at the end of each unit, offering supplementary grammar or writing skill development.

Learning Logs ask students to catalog the vocabulary, grammar, and life skills they have learned, and determine which areas they need to review.

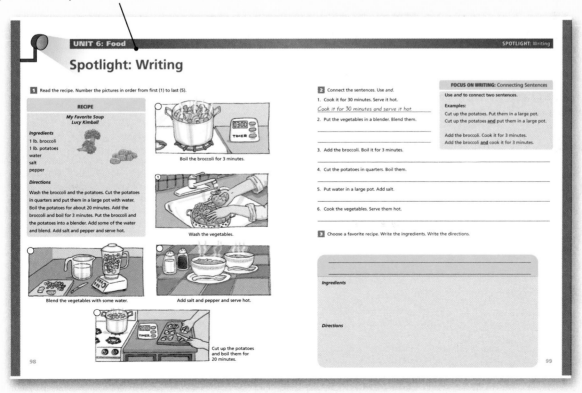

INTRODUCTION

What's your name?

1 Practice the Conversation 🎧

Listen to the conversation. Then listen and repeat.

A: Hello. My name is Anna .

B: Hi. I'm Tom .

A: Nice to meet you, Tom .

B: Nice to meet you, too.

Practice the conversation with 3 classmates.

2 Say the Alphabet 🎧

Listen to the letters. Then listen and repeat.

A a	B b	C c	D d
E e	F f	G g	H h
I i	J j	K k	L l
M m	N n	O o	P p
Q q	R r	S s	T t
U u	V v	W w	X x
Y y	Z z		

3 Practice the Conversation 🎧

Listen to the conversation. Then listen and repeat.

A: What's your first name?

B: Sue .

A: What's your last name?

B: Chan .

A: How do you spell that?

B: C-h-a-n .

Ask 6 classmates. Write their answers below.

FIRST NAME (GIVEN NAME)	LAST NAME (FAMILY NAME)
Sue	Chan

4 Write

Read Sue's name tag. Make a name tag for yourself.

Hi. My name is

Sue Chan

Hi. My name is

Where are you from?

THINGS TO DO

1 Find the Countries 🎧

Look at the map. Listen to the words. Then listen and repeat.

① Canada ⑦ France

② the United States ⑧ Morocco

③ Mexico ⑨ Somalia

④ Haiti ⑩ China

⑤ Colombia ⑪ Vietnam

⑥ Brazil ⑫ _____

Write the name of one more country. Find it on the map.

2 Ask Questions 🎧

Listen to the conversation. Then listen and repeat.

A: What's your name?

B: My name is Victor .

A: Where are you from?

B: I am from Mexico .

A: Mexico ! That's interesting.

Ask 4 classmates: What's your name? Where are you from? Write their answers below.

WHAT'S YOUR NAME?	WHERE ARE YOU FROM?
Victor	Mexico

3 Write

Write about 4 classmates.

EXAMPLE: Victor is from Mexico .

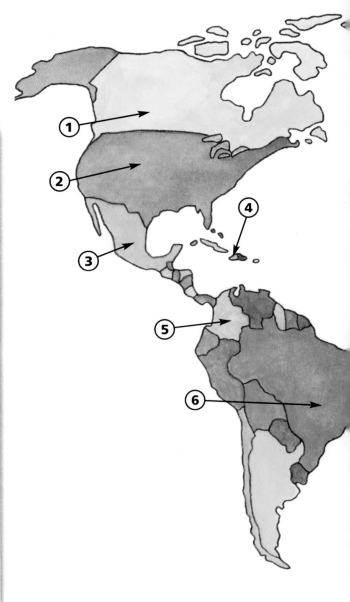

★ ★

TRY THIS Name a country that begins with each letter of the alphabet.

EXAMPLE: A: Australia
B: Brazil
C: _____

★ ★

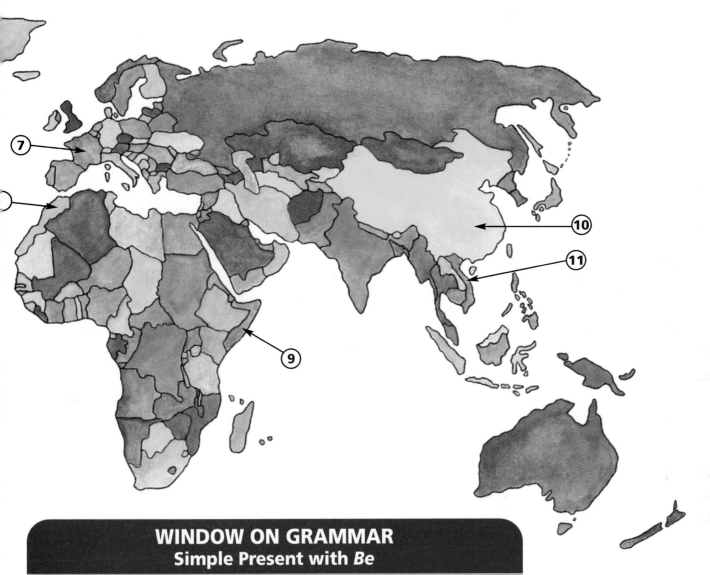

WINDOW ON GRAMMAR
Simple Present with *Be*

 Read the sentences.

I am from China.	You **are** from Japan.	He **is** from Brazil.
	We **are** from Haiti.	She **is** from France.
	They **are** from Mexico.	It **is** from Canada.

B Complete the sentences with *am, is,* or *are.*

1. Victor _____ from Mexico.
2. Victor and I _____ from Mexico.
3. Sandra _____ from Colombia.
4. I _____ from Vietnam.
5. You _____ from Somalia.
6. New York _____ in the United States.

2 LESSON

Where's your notebook?

THINGS TO DO

1 Learn New Words 🎧

Look at the picture. Listen to the words. Then listen and repeat.

① teacher	⑥ table	⑪ pencil	⑮ chair
② wall	⑦ calendar	⑫ piece of paper	⑯ computer
③ clock	⑧ map		⑰ desk
④ door	⑨ notebook	⑬ book	⑱ student
⑤ board	⑩ pen	⑭ floor	⑲ window

2 Write

What's in your classroom? Write 5 things. Then share your ideas with the class.

clock	

3 Ask Questions

Work with a partner. Ask and answer questions about the picture.

A: Where's

the map?	the computer?
the book?	the _____?

B: It's

on the wall.	on the table.
on the desk.	_____.

★ ★

 TRY THIS Make vocabulary flash cards like this.

(Front)   (Back) chair

Use your flash cards to learn new words.

★ ★

3 LESSON

Read page 6.

THINGS TO DO

1 Learn New Words 🎧

Look at the pictures. Listen to the classroom instructions. Then listen and repeat.

2 Follow Instructions

Work with a partner. Take turns giving 5 instructions.

A: Raise your hand.

3 Write

Write <u>your own</u> instructions. Then give an instruction to the class.

1. Say _hello._____
2. Write _____
3. Open _____
4. Close _____
5. Go to _____

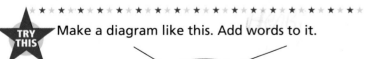

★ ★

TRY THIS Make a diagram like this. Add words to it.

Things that open and close

door

★ ★

① Read page 10.

② Listen to the words.

⑦ Write your name.

⑧ Practice the conversation with a partner.

⑬ Stand up.

⑭ Sit down.

8

③ Repeat the words.

④ Say *computer.*

⑤ Ask a partner.

⑥ Circle your name.

⑨ Take out a piece of paper.

⑩ Open your book.

⑪ Close the window.

⑫ Raise your hand.

⑮ Go to the board.

WINDOW ON MATH 🎧
Numbers 0 to 11

A Listen to the numbers. Then listen and repeat.

0 zero	1 one	2 two	3 three
4 four	5 five	6 six	7 seven
8 eight	9 nine	10 ten	11 eleven

B Listen to the conversation. Then listen and repeat.

A: Open your book to page 5 .
B: Which page?
A: Page 5 .
Practice the conversation with a partner.
Use different numbers.

4
LESSON

Application Forms

THINGS TO DO

1 Learn New Words 🎧

Look at the picture. Listen to the information. Then listen and repeat.

1. middle name
2. address
3. street
4. city
5. state
6. zip code
7. telephone number
8. area code
9. birthplace
10. gender
11. male
12. female
13. marital status
14. single
15. married
16. divorced
17. occupation

2 Read

Read the application form. Complete the sentences below.

Paul's _____ _last_ _____ _name_ _____ is Bridges. His

_____ _____ is Richard. His _____ is

8517 Alvarado Street in Los Angeles, California. The _____

_____ is 91012. Paul's _____ _____

is (310) 555-5678. His _____ is the U.S.

3 Write

Work with a partner.

Ask questions.

Write your partner's answers on the form.

EXAMPLE: What's your <u>first name</u>?

Application Form

Name _Henri_ _Arnoldo_ _Cobbadres_
       First   Middle   Last

Address _11206 EVONS TRL_ _BeltsviLLE_ _M.D_ _20705_
        Street   City   State   Zip Code

Telephone Number _240_ _751. 0107_
              Area Code

Birthplace _en el solvodor_

Gender: ☐ Male ☒ Female   Marital Status: ☐ Single ☒ Married ☐ Divorced

Occupation _corpinter_

Application Form

(PLEASE PRINT)

Name ① Paul ③ Richard ④ Bridges
First   Middle   Last ⑥

② Address 8517 Alvarado St., LosAngeles, ⑤ CA 91012
Street   City   State   Zip Code

⑦ Telephone Number ⑧ (310) 555-5678
Area Code

⑨ Birthplace Sacramento, CA, U.S.

⑩ Gender: ⑪ ☑ Male ⑫ ☐ Female Marital Status: ⑬ ☐ Single ⑮ ☑ Married ⑯ ☐ Divorced

⑰ Occupation teacher

WINDOW ON GRAMMAR
Punctuation Marks

period (.)	comma (,)	question mark (?)

A Circle the punctuation marks.

1. Where are you from?
2. I am from Miami, Florida.
3. Your book is on the floor.
4. Where is Paris, France?

B Add the punctuation marks.

1. What's her name?
2. Listen to your teacher.
3. He is from San Francisco, California.
4. His birthplace is Toronto, Canada.

Nice to meet you.

1 Practice the Conversation: Greeting Someone 🎧

Listen to the conversation. Then listen and repeat.

A: Hello . I'm Mr. Campos.

B: Nice to meet you, Mr. Campos.
   I'm Ms. Jones .

A: Nice to meet you.

Practice the conversation with a partner.
Use these items.

1 Hi.	2 How do you do?
Mrs. Lee	Mrs. Bridges

3 Hello.	4 How do you do?
Ms. Kim	Mr. Thomas

Mr. = a single or married male
Ms. = a single or married female
Mrs. = a married female

2 Practice the Conversation: Introducing Someone 🎧

Listen to the conversation. Then listen and repeat.

A: Hi, Jon. How are you?

B: Fine , thanks. And you?

A: I'm fine. Jon, this is my friend Gina.

B: Hi, Gina. Nice to meet you.

Practice the conversation with a partner.
Use these items.

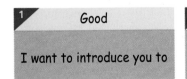

1 Good
I want to introduce you to

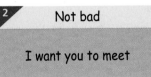

2 Not bad
I want you to meet

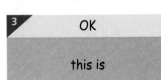

3 OK
this is

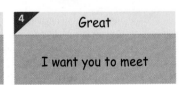

4 Great
I want you to meet

3 Practice the Conversation: Saying Good-bye 🎧

Listen to the conversation. Then listen and repeat.

A: Good-bye, Jon.

B: Bye, David. Have a nice day.

A: You too.

Practice the conversation with a partner.
Use these items.

1 See you later.	2 Nice to see you.	3 Have a great day.	4 Have a good day.
Have a nice day.	Nice to see you, too.	OK, you too.	Thanks, you too.

WINDOW ON PRONUNCIATION 🎧
Long Vowel Sounds: *I* and *E*

 Listen to the words. Then listen and repeat.

1. I	4. me	7. my	10. he	13. we	16. read
2. fine	5. meet	8. try	11. street	14. write	17. bye
3. see	6. hi	9. three	12. China	15. nice	18. country

 Write the words in the correct place.

Sounds like *I*		Sounds like *E*	
I		see	
fine		me	

 Listen and circle the word you hear.

1. (my) me		3. I E		5. bye B
2. hi he		4. write read		6. Y we

13

Occupations

1 Learn New Words 🎧

Look at the pictures below. Listen to the words. Then listen and repeat.

① Joan Baxter is a **dentist**.

② Larry Fisher is a **bus driver**.

③ Ken Park is a **pharmacist**.

④ Emma Lambert is a **doctor**.

⑤ Paul Ming is a **salesclerk**.

⑥ David Campos is a **machinist**.

⑦ Gina Mata is a **police officer**.

⑧ Leo Brunov is a **nurse**.

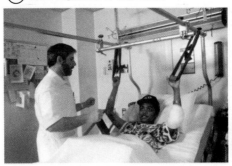

⑨ Amy Craft is a **cashier**.

2 Ask Questions

Work with a partner. Ask about the people above.

A: What's Joan's occupation?

B: She's a dentist.

Possessives
Add 's to a
person's name.

14

3 Read

Read the ads and circle the occupations.

JOB ADS

1
4 Day Work Week
BUS DRIVER
Earn $14/hr
Please call
916–555–0819
for an interview.

2
Immediate Openings
for 3 Machinists.
Apply at:
J&D Machine Co.
433 Ray Avenue
Auburn, California
916–202–1234

3
SALESCLERK
Experienced. Must
Work Weekends.
Food for Pets.
11 Alvarado Street
555–7400

4
CASHIER WANTED
Work 3 days a week.
Apply in person:
Shop and Go
873 Mission Street
916–682–1414

5
Smith Drugstore
needs a Pharmacist
for their Sacramento
store. Call for an
interview:
916–555–8700

6
DRIVER, Tow
Truck full time.
Must live in Davis,
experience necessary.
10 Johnson Road
916–555–0612

4 Write

Write the occupations. Then write the street address or telephone number from each job ad.

OCCUPATION	STREET ADDRESS	TELEPHONE NUMBER
1. Bus driver	XXX	(916) 555-0819
2. mochists	433 Roy Avenue	916 - 202 - 1234
3. SolesClERK	11 Alvorado street	(301) 555 - 7400
4. CaSHiER wantED	Mission street	916 - 682 - 1414
5. PhARhmasist	XXX	916 555 8700
6. DrivER	10 Johnson Road	916 -555 - 0612

15

7 LESSON

What do you know?

1 Listening Review 🎧

Listen and choose the correct answer. Use the Answer Sheet below.

1.

A   B   C

2.

 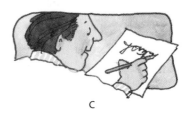

A   B   C

3.

A   B   C

4.

A   B   C

5. A. 22 Long Street
   B. 555-5498
   C. 03550

6. A. 212
   B. 54356
   C. 555-5683

7. A. She's from Haiti.
   B. female
   C. She's a police officer.

8. A. Los Angeles
   B. California
   C. Mexico

9. A. 22
   B. 508
   C. 555-2494

10. A. 10 Main Street
    B. 423
    C. 555-5428

ANSWER SHEET

1 (A) (B) (C)
2 (A) (B) (C)
3 (A) (B) (C)
4 (A) (B) (C)
5 (A) (B) (C)
6 (A) (B) (C)
7 (A) (B) (C)
8 (A) (B) (C)
9 (A) (B) (C)
10 (A) (B) (C)

2 Conversation Check: Pair Work

Student A: Go to page 164.

Student B: Ask your partner questions to complete this chart. Write the answers.

EXAMPLE:　**B:** What is Don's last name?

　　　　　A: Garcia.

First Name	Last Name	Gender	Occupation	Telephone Number
1. Don	Garcia	M	Police Officer	(545) 555-5943
2. Gloria	Ramos	F	Nurse	
3. Van	Pham	F		(943) 555-5873
4.	Smith	M	Cashier	(543) 555-9004
5. Victor	Abarca	M		(359) 555-4833

✔

How many questions did you ask your partner?	How many questions did you answer?
☐ 1　☐ 2　☐ 3　☐ 4　☐ 5	☐ 1　☐ 2　☐ 3　☐ 4　☐ 5

✔ LEARNING LOG

I know these words:

☐ address	☐ country	☐ male	☐ period	☐ student
☐ am	☐ dentist	☐ map	☐ pharmacist	☐ table
☐ are	☑ desk	☐ marital status	☑ piece of paper	☐ take out
☐ area code	☐ divorced	☐ married	☐ police officer	☐ teacher
☐ ask	☐ doctor	☐ middle name	☐ practice	☐ telephone
☑ birthplace	☐ door	☐ Mr.	☐ question mark	number
☐ board	☐ eight	☐ Mrs.	☐ raise	☐ ten
☐ book	☐ eleven	☐ Ms.	☑ read	☐ three
☐ bus driver	☐ female	☑ nine	☐ repeat	☐ two
☐ calendar	☐ fine	☐ notebook	☑ salesclerk	☐ wall
☐ cashier	☐ five	☐ nurse	☐ say	☐ window
☑ chair	☐ floor	☐ occupation	☐ seven	☑ write
☐ circle	☐ four	☐ one	☐ single	☐ zero
☐ city	☐ gender	☐ open	☐ sit down	☐ zip code
☐ clock	☐ go to	☐ partner	☐ six	
☐ close	☐ is	☐ pen	☐ stand up	
☐ comma	☐ listen	☐ pencil	☐ state	
☐ computer	☐ machinist	☐ people	☐ street	

I can ask:

☐ What's your name?
☐ Where are you from?
☐ Where's your book?
☑ How do you do?

I can say:

☐ I am from Mexico.
☐ That's interesting!
☐ It's on the table.
☐ Open your book.
☐ This is my friend, Gina.
☐ Have a nice day.

I can write:

☐ personal information
☐ telephone numbers
☐ zip codes
☐ street addresses
☐ numbers 0 to 11

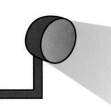

Spotlight: Grammar

SIMPLE PRESENT OF *BE*				
Affirmative		Negative	Contractions Affirmative	Negative
I **am** from China.		I **am not** from China.	I'm	I'm not
You **are** from China. We **are** from China. They **are** from China.		You **are not** from China. We **are not** from China. They **are not** from China.	You're We're They're	You aren't We aren't They aren't
He **is** from China. She **is** from China. It **is** from China.		He **is not** from China. She **is not** from China. It **is not** from China.	He's She's It's	He isn't She isn't It isn't

1 Read the story. Circle 16 examples of the simple present of *be*.

There (are) twenty (20) students in my class. Ten students (are) from Mexico. Four students (are) from Russia. Three students are from China. (Two) students (are) from Haiti, and one student is (from) Egypt. Eleven students in my class (are) married. Nine students (are) single. I (am) the student from Egypt. My name (is) Fatima, and I (am) married. My teacher (is) Mr. White. (His) first name (is) David, and he (is) from Canada. Mr. White (is) not married. He (is) single.

2 Read the story again. Complete the sentences with *are, is, are not,* and *is not*.

1. Fatima ___is not___ from Russia. She ___is___ from Egypt.

2. Fatima ___is not___ married. She ___is not___ single.

3. Eleven students in Fatima's class ___are___ married.

4. Mr. White ___is not___ a bus driver. He ___is___ a teacher.

5. Mr. White and Fatima ___are not___ from the United States.

6. Mr. White ___is not___ from Egypt. He ___is___ from Canada.

7. Two students in Fatima's class ___are___ from Haiti.

3 Rewrite each sentence above. Use contractions.

EXAMPLE: *Fatima isn't from Russia. She's from Egypt.*

POSSESSIVE ADJECTIVES: *my, your, our, their, her, his*

my book	your book	our book	their book	her book	his book

POSSESSIVES WITH NAMES

John's book is here.

Tina's book is on the table.

Mr. White's book is on the desk.

John and Tina's teacher is Mr. White.

Andy's address is on the application form.

Ms. Jones's zip code is 94704.

4 Complete the sentences. Write *my, your, our, their, his,* or *her.*

1. Ling and Bob live in Pasadena. _____*Their*_____ address is 5434 N. Wilson Avenue.

2. Tina and I are students. _____*Our,*_____ school is on Altadena Drive.

3. My teacher's first name is John. _____*his,*_____ middle name is Frank.

4. I live in New York. _____*my,*_____ telephone number is (212) 555-5439.

5. Anna is not married. _____*her.*_____ marital status is single.

6. Mr. Santos and Ms. Jones are teachers. _____*Ther*_____ students are in _____*Ther*_____ classrooms.

5 Write a sentence about each person.

1. Bob/telephone number/555-9584

   Bob's telephone number is 555-9584.

2. David/zip code/91012

   _____

3. Rose/marital status/married

   _____

4. Anna/area code/212

   _____

5. Mr. White/first name/David

   _____

2 LESSON

It's next to the drugstore.

THINGS TO DO

1 Learn New Words 🎧

Look at the pictures. Listen to the words. Then listen and repeat.

① next to   ④ in front of   ⑥ in back of
② between   ⑤ near   ⑦ on the corner of
③ across from   *cerca*

Write the words on the pictures.

2 Practice the Conversation 🎧

Listen to the conversation. Then listen and repeat.

A: Excuse me. Where's the post office ?
B: It's next to the drugstore .
A: Next to the drugstore ?
B: That's right.

Practice the conversation with a partner. Ask about each picture.

3 Write

Work with a partner. Find the places in pictures 1 to 7 on the map.

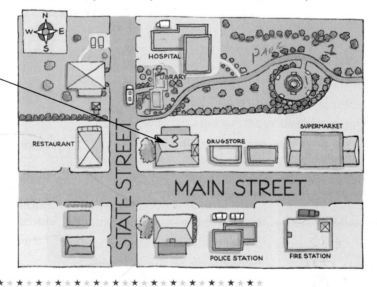

EXAMPLE: The post office is here.

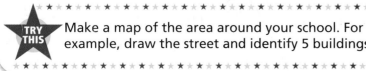

TRY THIS — Make a map of the area around your school. For example, draw the street and identify 5 buildings.

(1)

The post office is _____ next _____ to _____ the drugstore

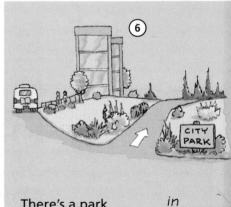

(4)

The bookmobile is

_____ in _____
back of
The librori

the library.

(6)

There's a park _____ in _____
on of
bACk _____ the library

22

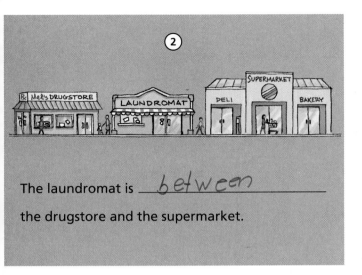

The laundromat is ___between___

the drugstore and the supermarket.

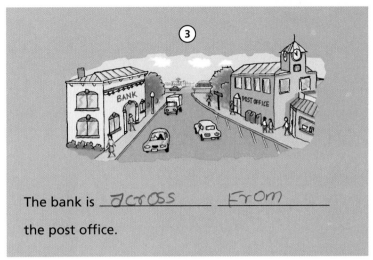

The bank is ___across___ ___From___

the post office.

The school is ___near___

the park.

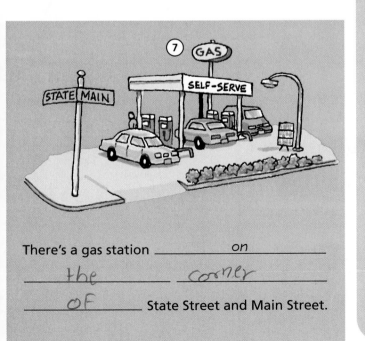

There's a gas station _____on_____

____the____ ____corner____

____oF____ State Street and Main Street.

WINDOW ON GRAMMAR
Is there/Are there

A Read the sentences.

QUESTIONS	ANSWERS
Is there a bank on Third Street?	Yes, there is.
Is there a school on Third Street?	No, there isn't.
Are there parks in town?	Yes, there are.
Are there movie theaters in town?	No, there aren't.

B Complete the sentences with *Is there* or *Are there*. Then ask a partner.

1. ___is there___ a supermarket near your home?
2. ___is there___ a community center near your home?
3. ___is there___ gas stations in your town?
4. ___is there___ a bank across from your home?
5. ___is there___ good restaurants near your home?
6. ___ARe there___ two movie theaters on your street?

23

Is there an ATM around here?

THINGS TO DO

1 Talk About the Picture

Write 5 things about the picture. Share your ideas with the class.

> EXAMPLES: There's a post office on Pine Street.
> There's a restaurant next to the drugstore.

2 Learn New Words 🎧

Look at the picture. Listen to the words. Then listen and repeat.

① **bus stop**	⑧ **stoplight**	⑮ **no parking**
② **parking lot**	⑨ **truck**	⑯ **do not enter**
③ **bus**	⑩ **taxi**	⑰ **no right turn**
④ **ambulance**	⑪ **car**	⑱ **no left turn**
⑤ **crosswalk**	⑫ **pay phone**	⑲ **one way**
⑥ **sidewalk**	⑬ **ATM**	
⑦ **mailbox**	⑭ **stop**	

3 Practice the Conversation 🎧

Listen to the conversation. Then listen and repeat.

A: Excuse me. Is there a mailbox around here?

B: Yes, there is. There's one on Pine Street. It's in front of the post office .

A: Thanks a lot.

Practice the conversation with a partner. Ask about these things.

in front of / ?

in front of / ?

next to / ?

near / ?

between / ?

across from / ?

Maps

THINGS TO DO

1 Talk About the Picture

Answer the questions.

QUESTIONS	ANSWERS
a. What states are next to Florida?	*Alabama and Georgia*
b. What states are next to California?	
c. What state is between Texas and Arizona?	
d. Where is the city of Atlanta?	

Write 3 questions about places in the U.S. Ask a partner your questions.

2 Learn New Words 🎧

Look at the map. Listen to the words. Then listen and repeat.

① capital   ③ south of   ⑤ west of

② north of   ④ east of

Write the words on the lines below.

1. The _____*capital*_____ of Florida is Tallahassee.
2. New York is ___north of___ Pennsylvania.
3. Texas is ___south of___ Oklahoma.
4. Texas is ___east of___ New Mexico.
5. Arizona is ___west of___ New Mexico.

3 Read

Read and answer the questions.

1.	2.
This state is north of Alabama and south of Kentucky. The capital of this state is Nashville. What state is it?	This state is east of Utah and west of Kansas. The capital of this state is Denver. What state is it?
_____	_____

0 0 50 estados

Montana · North Dakota · Minnesota · Wisconsin · Michigan (Lansing) · New Hampshire · Maine · Vermont · Massachusetts · Boston · New York · Albany · Rhode Island · Connecticut · Trenton · New Jersey · Delaware · Maryland · West Virginia · Pennsylvania · Virginia · South Dakota · Wyoming · Nebraska · Iowa · Illinois (Springfield) · Indiana · Ohio · Kentucky · North Carolina · Denver · Colorado · Kansas · Missouri · Tennessee (Nashville) · South Carolina · New Mexico · Oklahoma · Arkansas · Atlanta · Georgia · Texas · Mississippi · Alabama · Tallahassee · Louisiana · Austin · Florida

N ② W ⑤ E ④ S ③

WINDOW ON MATH 🎧
Reading Math Symbols

A Read the symbols.

+ plus (and)	= equals	> is more than
– minus		< is less than

B Read the sentences.

1 + 2 = 3   3 – 2 = 1   6 > 5   8 < 9

C Add the missing symbols.

1. 5 **+** 1 **=** 6   3. 7 **>** 3   5. 1 **−** 1 **=** 0

2. 3 **+** 2 **<** 5   4. 2 **<** 4   6. 4 **+** 2 **=** 6

27

Is there a restaurant near here?

1 Practice the Conversation: Asking for Repetition 🎧

Listen to the conversation. Then listen and repeat.

A: Is there a restaurant near here?

B: Excuse me?

A: Is there a restaurant near here?

B: Yes, there is. There's one on Pine.

A: Thanks.

Practice the conversation with a partner. Use these items.

1 a supermarket	2 an ATM	3 a bank	4
I'm sorry, what was that?	Please say that again.	What was that?	

2 Practice the Conversation: Saying You Don't Know 🎧

Listen to the conversation. Then listen and repeat.

A: Excuse me. Is there a drugstore near here?

B: I'm not sure.

A: Okay. Thanks anyway.

Practice the conversation with a partner. Use these items.

1 a gas station	2 a parking lot	3 a laundromat	4
Sorry, I don't know.	Sorry, I'm new in town.	Sorry, I'm not sure.	

3 Practice the Conversation: Asking a Follow-Up Question 🎧

Listen to the conversation. Then listen and repeat.

A: Where's Sacramento ?

B: It's in California .

A: In the north or south of the state?

B: In the north .

Practice the conversation with a partner. Use these items.

1	Atlanta
	Georgia/north

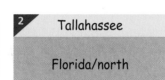

2	Tallahassee
	Florida/north

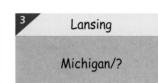

3	Lansing
	Michigan/?

WINDOW ON PRONUNCIATION 🎧
Voiced and Voiceless *Th* Sounds

A Listen to the words. Then listen and repeat.

1. thanks	3. there	5. theater	7. three	9. the	11. they
2. then	4. third	6. that	8. this	10. north	12. south

Write the words in the correct place.

Th sounds like *thanks*		*Th* sounds like *the*	
thanks	_____	the	_____
_____	_____	_____	_____
_____	_____	_____	_____

B Work with a partner. Ask and answer the questions.

1. What is 1 plus 2?

2. Is there a bank near the school?

3. Is the United States north or south of Mexico?

4. Is the United States north or south of Canada?

5. Where is the theater?

6

LESSON

The Public Library

1 Learn New Words 🎧

Look at the pictures. Listen to the words. Then listen and repeat.

1. librarian
2. checkout desk
3. library card
4. magazines
5. audiobooks
6. videos
7. children's books

Write the words on the lines.

1. *librarian*
2. *checkout desk*
3. *library card*

Edwards Public Library
42 Linsdale Ave.
Springfield, Illinois

No._____ Name_____

Present this card each time you borrow a book.
You are responsible for books borrowed on this card.

How do I get a library card?
Go to the checkout desk and complete
an application. Your card is free.

4. *magazines*
5. *audio books*
6. *videos*

What can I take out from the library?
You can take out books, magazines,
audiobooks, and videos.

30

What's in the library for children?
There are lots of books for
children. There is also a
story-telling program.

⑦ _children's books_

Are there any computers in the library?
Yes, there are. You can use the computers in the library.

2 Write

Complete this library card application form.

Edwards Public Library

Application for an Adult Library Card

Part 1 Please print clearly. Enter only one letter or number per box.

| C | o | l | i | n | d | r | e | s | | | r | e | s | | | | | | |

Last Name

| H | E | N | R | i | | | | | |

First Name

| A | r | n | o | l | d | o | | | |

Middle Name or Initial

| 1 | 1 | 2 | 0 | 6 | E | v | a | n | s | | T | R | L | | | | | | |

Street Address

| 0 | 0 | I | |

Apt.#

| B | e | l | T | S | v | i | l | l | E | | | | |

City

| M | D |

State

| 2 | 0 | 7 | 0 | 5 |

Zip Code

| 2 | 4 | 0 |

Area Code

| 7 | 5 | 1 | 0 | 1 | 0 | 7 |

Phone Number

Email address

Part 2 Please choose an easy-to-remember four-digit Personal Identification Number (PIN).

Numbers only, no letters.

| 0 | 5 | 0 | 8 |

Part 3 Please read the statement and then sign your name.

I agree to be responsible for all materials borrowed against my Edwards Public Library card. I will notify the library immediately if my address changes or if my card is lost.

Signature

★ ★

TRY THIS Go to your public library. Write 5 things you see.

★ ★

7 LESSON

What do you know?

1 Listening Review 🎧

Listen and choose the correct place. Use the Answer Sheet.

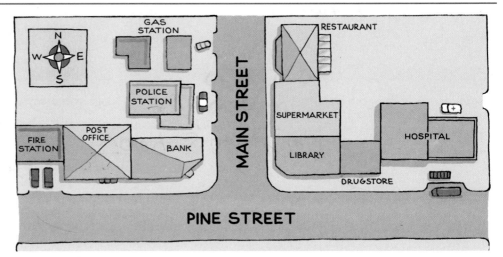

1. A. the police station
   B. the drugstore
   c. the fire station

2. A. the bank
   B. the fire station
   c. the supermarket

3. A. the drugstore
   B. the fire station
   c. the library

4. A. the police station
   B. the bank
   c. the supermarket

5. A. the hospital
   B. the post office
   c. the gas station

6. A. the restaurant
   B. the library
   c. the police station

ANSWER SHEET

1	(A)	(B)	(C)
2	(A)	(B)	(C)
3	(A)	(B)	(C)
4	(A)	(B)	(C)
5	(A)	(B)	(C)
6	(A)	(B)	(C)

2 Dictation 🎧

Listen and write the words you hear.

1. A: Excuse me. _Where's the_ _____?
   B: It's on Front Street.

2. A: Excuse me. _____ near here?
   B: Yes, there is. It's in front of the library.

3. A: _____ of New Mexico?
   B: I'm not sure.

3 Conversation Check: Pair Work

Student A: Go to page 164.

Student B: Ask your partner the 2 questions below. Mark the places on the map.

1. Where's the post office?

2. Where's the bank?

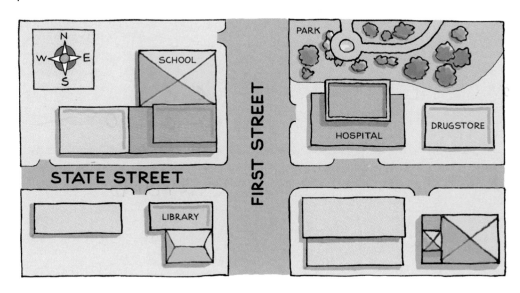

 ✔

How many questions did you ask your partner?	How many questions did you answer?
☐ 1 ☐ 2	▣ 1 ▣ 2

✔ LEARNING LOG

I know these words:

☐ across from	☐ children's book	☐ laundromat	☐ next to	☐ school
☐ ambulance	☐ community center	☐ left	☐ north	☑ sidewalk
☐ ATM	☐ crosswalk	☑ less than	☐ on the corner of	☐ south
☐ audiobook	☐ drugstore	☐ librarian	☐ one way	☐ stop
☐ bank	☐ east	☐ library	☐ park	☑ stoplight
☐ between	☐ enter	☐ library card	☐ parking lot	☐ supermarket
☐ bookmobile	☐ equals	☐ magazine	☐ pay phone	☐ taxi
☐ bus	☐ fire station	☐ mailbox	☐ plus	☐ truck
☐ bus stop	☐ gas station	☑ minus	☐ police station	☐ turn
☐ capital	☐ hospital	☐ more than	☐ post office	☐ video
☐ car	☐ in back of	☐ movie theater	☐ restaurant	☐ west
☐ checkout desk	☐ in front of	☐ near	☑ right	

I can ask:

☐ Where's the post office?
☐ Is there a restaurant near here?
☐ Excuse me?

I can say:

☐ The library is next to the police station.
☐ There's a supermarket on Pine Street.
☐ There are five movie theaters near here.
☐ 5 + 3 = 8

I can write:

☐ an application for a library card

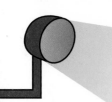

Spotlight: Writing

1 Read stories A and B below. Find these words.

Find the words with C.
c _a_ _r_ _o_ _l_
c _o_ _l_ _e_ _r_ _a_ _d_ _o_
c _a_ _r_
c _l_ _e_ _a_ _n_

Find the words with R.
r _e_ _a_ _d_
R _e_ _n_ _o_
r _a_ _d_ _i_ _o_
r _o_ _o_ _m_

STORIES 🎧

A.

Hi! My name is Carol. I'm from Colorado. I like to read, talk on the telephone, and go to the movies. I don't like to watch TV.

B.

My name is David. I'm from Reno, Nevada. I like to drive my car, listen to the radio, and go to parties. I don't like to clean my room.

2 Correct the story. Add 5 punctuation marks.

My name is Ann. I like to watch
TV, read books, and go to school. I don't
like to go to the supermarket.

> **FOCUS ON WRITING:** Punctuation Marks
>
> • Use a period (.) at the end of a sentence.
>   *Example:* He's a doctor.
>
> • Use a comma (,) between words in a series.
>   *Example:* I like to read, go to the library,
>   and go to the park.

3 Complete the chart about you. Use the words below. Then add 3 more activities.

dance

I like to	I don't like to
dance	
I like fo	

go to the dentist

relax

eat

wash dishes

4 Write your own story.

My name is _Henri. I like to go to_
school.
I don't like movies.
I like to go to library.
I like to look at magazine.
I like to watch TV.

> *Add your picture here.*

35

LESSON 2

Is the library open on Monday?

THINGS TO DO

1 Talk About the Picture

Write 5 things about the picture.

EXAMPLE: There are people in front of the library.

Share your ideas with the class.

2 Learn New Words 🎧

Listen and repeat the words.

① Sunday   ⑤ Thursday   ⑧ No smoking.

② Monday   ⑥ Friday   ⑨ No eating.

③ Tuesday   ⑦ Saturday

④ Wednesday

Find the words and signs in the picture.

3 Practice the Conversation 🎧

Listen to the conversation. Then listen and repeat.

A: Is the library open on Monday ?

B: Yes, it's open from noon to 9:00.

A: From noon to 9:00 ?

B: Right.

Closed =
Not Open

Practice the conversation with a partner. Use these items.

¹ Tuesday	² Wednesday	³ Saturday	⁴
10 A.M. to 9 P.M.	noon to 9 P.M.	10 A.M. to 5 P.M.	

★ ★

TRY THIS Write the hours of your library or school.

EXAMPLE: Sunday   9:00 A.M. to 5:00 P.M.
             Monday   9:00 A.M. to 7:00 P.M.

★ ★

3 LESSON

It's five cents.

Coins

THINGS TO DO

1 Learn New Words 🎧

Look at the pictures. Listen to the words. Then listen and repeat.

① penny   ⑤ half-dollar   ⑨ twenty dollars

② nickel   ⑥ dollar   ⑩ fifty dollars

③ dime   ⑦ five dollars   ⑪ one hundred dollars

④ quarter   ⑧ ten dollars   ⑫ one thousand dollars

Write the words under the pictures.

2 Write

Add the coins.

1. _____thirty-five cents (35¢)_____

2. _____

3. _____

4. _____

3 Practice the Conversation 🎧

Listen to the conversation. Then listen and repeat.

A: How much is it?

B: Thirty cents .

A: Are you sure?

B: Yes.

Practice the conversation with a partner. Ask about the 4 items in Activity 2.

① a _____penny_____
(one cent/1¢)

② a _____
(five cents/5¢)

③ a _____
(ten cents/10¢)

④ a _____
(twenty-five cents/25¢)

⑤ a _____
(fifty cents/50¢)

Bills

⑥ a _____
($1.00)

⑦ _____
($5.00)

⑧ _____
($10.00)

⑨ _____
($20.00)

⑩ _____
($50.00)

⑪ _____
($100.00)

⑫ _____
($1,000.00)

WINDOW ON GRAMMAR
Questions with *How much*

A Read the questions and answers.

QUESTIONS	ANSWERS
How much is it?	It's fifty cents.
How much is the pen?	It's one dollar.
How much is a late book?	It's five cents a day.

B Work with a partner. Ask and answer 5 questions.

How much is	a penny	and	a penny?
	a nickel		a nickel?
	a dime		a dime?
	a quarter		a quarter?
	a dollar		a dollar?
	_____		_____?

EXAMPLE: A: How much is a penny and a quarter?
  B: It's twenty-six cents (26¢).

41

Checks

4
LESSON

THINGS TO DO

1 Learn New Words 🎧

Look at the pictures. Listen to the words. Then listen and repeat.

① **check**　　② **check number**　　③ **amount**　　④ **signature**

2 Read

Complete this chart with information from the 3 checks.

Check #	To	Amount	For
124	Coral Beach Library	$12.00	late books
125			

3 Write

Write the check amounts.

1. $25.00 　　　_Twenty-five and ^{00}/100 dollars_
2. $31.50 　　　_____
3. $56.34 　　　_____

Write a check to Ace Drugstore for $53.10.

```
DAVID CAMPOS                                        127
35 Hay St., Apt. 3C
Coral Beach, FL 33915          DATE_____

PAY TO THE
ORDER OF_____  $ [        ]

_____ DOLLARS

TRUE BANK
Florida

MEMO_____    _____
⑈:012345678⑈:   123⑈456 7⑈  0127
```

★ ★

TRY THIS　Draw a check. Then write a check for something you want.

★ ★

①

```
DAVID CAMPOS
35 Hay St., Apt. 3C
Coral Beach, FL 33915

PAY TO THE
ORDER OF  Coral Beac

Eighteen and  50/100
TRUE BANK
Florida

MEMO    for stamps
⑈:012345678⑈:    123⑈
```

② 124

DAVID CAMPOS
35 Hay St., Apt. 3C
Coral Beach, FL 33915

DATE 8/19/04

$ 12.00 ③

PAY TO THE
ORDER OF Coral Beach Library

Twelve and 00/100 _____ DOLLARS

TRUE BANK
Florida

D. Campos ④

MEMO for late books

⑂012345678⑂ 123⑁456 7⑁ 0124

DAVID CAMPOS
35 Hay St., Apt. 3C
Coral Beach, FL 33915

125

DATE 8/23/04

PAY TO THE
ORDER OF CASH

Fifty and 00/100 _____ $ 50.00

TRUE BANK
Florida

DOLLARS

MEMO for food

⑂012345678⑂ 123⑁456 7⑁ 0125

D. Campos

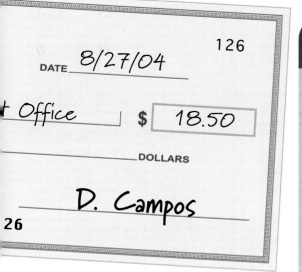

126

DATE 8/27/04

t Office $ 18.50

DOLLARS

D. Campos

26

WINDOW ON MATH
Adding and Subtracting

A Listen to the sentences. Then listen and repeat. 🎧

10¢ + 25¢ = 35¢	$1.00 + .50 = $1.50
50¢ + 25¢ = 75¢	$5.00 + $2.00 = $7.00
5¢ − 1¢ = 4¢	$10.00 − $1.00 = $9.00
60¢ − 10¢ = 50¢	$50.00 − $30.00 = $20.00

B Write the missing numbers. Read the sentences to a partner.

1. $3.00 − $1.50 = _____
2. $.75 − $.25 = _____
3. 50¢ + 10¢ = _____
4. $10.00 + $12.00 = _____
5. $5.00 + $10.00 = _____
6. $20.00 + $1.50 = _____
7. $100.00 − $20.00 = _____
8. $100.00 + $50.00 = _____

LESSON 5

Thank you for calling.

1 Practice the Conversation: Asking about Business Hours

Listen to the conversation. Then listen and repeat.

A: Hello. Anderson's Drugstore. Can I help you?

B: Yes. What are your hours on Thursday ?

A: We're open from 8:00 to 6:00 .

B: Thank you.

Practice the conversation with a partner. Use these items.

1 Saturday	2 Sunday	3 Tuesday	4 Wednesday	5
from 9:00 to noon	from noon to 7:00	from 9:00 to 9:00	from 9:00 to 9:00	💡

2 Practice the Conversation: Calling Directory Assistance

Listen to the conversation. Then listen and repeat.

A: Welcome to Horizon. What city and state?

B: Miami, Florida .

A: What listing?

B: Rafael Hernandez .

A: The number is area code 305-555-5938 .

Practice the conversation with a partner. Use these items.

1 New York, New York / Lisa Wu	2 Houston, Texas / Rita Smith	3 Santa Ana, California / Grace Chan	4 Miami, Florida / Shirley Garcia	5
212-555-8362	713-555-9146	714-555-2020	305-555-7864	💡

3 Listen and Write: Listening to a Recorded Message 🎧

Listen and write the missing numbers. Then listen and check.

Thank you for calling the Coral Beach Public Library. For hours, press 1.

The library is open Monday through Thursday

from _____11:00_____ to _____ .

On Friday and Saturday, the library is open

from _____ to _____ .

Good-bye.

WINDOW ON PRONUNCIATION 🎧
Thirteen or *Thirty*? Syllable Stress in Numbers

 Listen to the words. Then listen and repeat.

thirteen (13)	thirty (30)
fourteen (14)	forty (40)
fifteen (15)	fifty (50)
sixteen (16)	sixty (60)
seventeen (17)	seventy (70)
eighteen (18)	eighty (80)
nineteen (19)	ninety (90)

B Listen and circle the numbers you hear.

1. 13	30		5. 17	70
2. 14	40		6. 18	80
3. 15	50		7. 19	90
4. 16	60			

 Listen and point to the numbers you hear.

1. It's **six-fifty / six-fifteen**.

2. It's **fifteen / fifty** cents.

3. From **9:30 / 9:13** A.M. to 6:00 P.M.

4. The price is **$3.18 / $3.80**.

Listen as your partner says the numbers. Circle the numbers you hear.

COMMUNITY

6

LESSON

Business Hours

1 Read

Read the store signs. Answer the questions below.

WESTMINSTER BANK

Monday	9:00 a.m.–3:00 p.m.
Tuesday	9:00 a.m.–3:00 p.m.
Wednesday	9:00 a.m.–3:00 p.m.
Thursday	9:00 a.m.–3:00 p.m.
Friday	9:00 a.m.–3:00 p.m.
Saturday	**closed**
Sunday	**closed**

Johnson's Drugstore

Monday	7:30 a.m.–8:30 p.m.
Tuesday	7:30 a.m.–8:30 p.m.
Wednesday	7:30 a.m.–8:30 p.m.
Thursday	7:30 a.m.–8:30 p.m.
Friday	7:30 a.m.–8:30 p.m.
Saturday	8:30 a.m.–6:30 p.m.
Sunday	8:30 a.m.–6:30 p.m.

U.S. Post Office
Hours of Operation

Monday:	9–4
Tuesday:	9–4
Wednesday:	9–4
Thursday:	9–4
Friday:	9–4
Saturday:	9–2
Sunday:	**Closed**

ARMITAGE HOSPITAL VISITING HOURS

Open seven days a week.

Monday, Tuesday, Wednesday, Thursday, Friday, Saturday, Sunday

10 a.m.–12 p.m. & 7 p.m.–9 p.m.

1. What's open on Sunday morning? *The drugstore and the hospital are.* _____

2. When are both the bank and the post office open? _____

3. What's open every day? _____

4. What is closed on Sunday? _____

5. When's the post office open on Saturday? _____

6. It's 8:00 P.M. on Monday. What's open? _____

7. It's noon on Sunday. Is the bank open? _____

2 How Much Is It?

Study the pictures. Answer the questions.

1. How much is a telephone call? _____35¢_____

2. How much is it for two hours? _____

   How much is it for three hours? _____

3. How much is it for two hours? _____

   How much is it for three hours? _____

4. How much are two loads? _____

   How much are three loads? _____

3 Write

Find information about 3 places in your town. Then report to the class.

NAME	ADDRESS	TELEPHONE NUMBER	HOURS
State St. Bank	224 State Street	603–555–4873	Monday–Friday 9:00 – 4:00

7
LESSON

What do you know?

---

1 Listening Review 🎧

Listen and choose the time you hear. Use the Answer Sheet.

1.

      A   B   C

2.

      A   B   C

3.

      A   B   C

4.

      A   B   C

ANSWER SHEET		
1 (A)	(B)	(C)
2 (A)	(B)	(C)
3 (A)	(B)	(C)
4 (A)	(B)	(C)
5 (A)	(B)	(C)
6 (A)	(B)	(C)
7 (A)	(B)	(C)
8 (A)	(B)	(C)
9 (A)	(B)	(C)
10 (A)	(B)	(C)

Listen and choose the correct answer. Use the Answer Sheet.

5. A. 10:00 A.M.
   B. 9:00 to 5:00
   C. nine o'clock

6. A. It's nine o'clock.
   B. It's Friday.
   C. It's a quarter.

7. A. It's 1:00 A.M.
   B. It's ten cents.
   C. It's the library.

8. A. at 7:00
   B. $7.00
   C. at school

9. A. Yes, it is.
   B. on Monday
   C. Tuesday

10. A. three hundred dollars
    B. from 8:00 to 6:00
    C. at the library

2 Conversation Check: Pair Work

Student A: Go to page 165.

Student B: Ask your partner questions to complete this chart.

EXAMPLE: **B:** When is the community center open on Tuesday?

A: From noon to 8 P.M.

	Sunday	Monday	Tuesday	Wednesday	Thursday	Friday	Saturday
Community Center	closed	closed	noon to 8 P.M.	noon to 8 P.M.	noon to 8 P.M.	noon to 10 P.M.	
Laundromat	7 A.M. to 10 P.M.	noon to 10 P.M.	noon to 10 P.M.	10 A.M. to 10 P.M.	10 A.M. to 10 P.M.	10 A.M. to 10 P.M.	
Drugstore		8 A.M. to 9 P.M.	8 A.M. to 9 P.M.	8 A.M. to 9 P.M.	8 A.M. to 9 P.M.	8 A.M. to 9 P.M.	8 A.M. to 6 P.M.
Supermarket	8 A.M. to 8 P.M.	6 A.M. to midnight	6 A.M. to midnight	6 A.M. to midnight	6 A.M. to midnight		6 A.M. to 10 P.M.

| ✔ | How many questions did you ask your partner? □1 □2 □3 □4 □5 | How many questions did you answer? □1 □2 □3 □4 □5 |

✔ LEARNING LOG

I know these words:

□ after
□ afternoon
□ A.M.
□ amount
□ before
□ cents
□ check
□ check number
□ closed
□ day

□ dime
□ dollar
□ eighteen
□ eighty
□ evening
□ fifteen
□ fifty
□ forty
□ fourteen
□ Friday

□ half-dollar
□ hours
□ midnight
□ minute
□ Monday
□ morning
□ nickel
□ night
□ nineteen
□ ninety

□ noon
□ o'clock
□ open
□ penny
□ personal check
□ P.M.
□ quarter
□ Saturday
□ seventeen
□ seventy

□ signature
□ sixteen
□ sixty
□ smoking
□ Sunday
□ thirteen
□ thirty
□ thirty-five
□ thirty-one
□ Thursday

□ Tuesday
□ twelve
□ twenty
□ twenty-one
□ Wednesday
□ week

I can ask:

□ What time is it?
□ Is the library open on Sunday?
□ What are your hours?
□ How much is it?
□ Are you sure?

I can say:

□ It's two o'clock.
□ That's right.
□ It's open from noon to 9.
□ It's fifty cents.

I can write:

□ numbers 12 to 90
□ a personal check
□ amounts of money

49

Spotlight: Grammar

YES/NO QUESTIONS AND ANSWERS WITH _BE_		
_I_	_you, they_	_he, she, it_
<u>Am I</u> on State Street? Yes, **you are**. No, **you aren't** No, **you're not**.	<u>Are you</u> from Mexico? Yes, **I am**. No, **I am not**. No, **I'm not**. <u>Are you and Tina</u> from Canada? Yes, **we are**. No, **we aren't**. No, **we're not**. <u>Are the students</u> in class? Yes, **they are**. No, **they aren't**. No, **they're not**.	<u>Is Bob</u> a teacher? Yes, **he is**. No, **he isn't**. No, **he's not**. <u>Is Tina</u> a student? Yes, **she is**. No, **she isn't**. No, **she's not**. <u>Is your book</u> from China? Yes, **it is**. No, **it isn't**. No, **it's not**.

1 Write the words in the correct order. Then answer the questions.

1. A: _Are you from Mexico?_ _____ (you / from / Mexico / Are / ?)

   B: _____

2. A: _____ (your school / near a restaurant / Is / ?)

   B: _____

3. A: _____ (in the morning / Is / your class / ?)

   B: _____

4. A: _____ (five dollars / ten dollars / more than / Is / ?)

   B: _____

5. A: _____ (Are / your class / Don and Daisy / in / ?)

   B: _____

2 Complete the conversations. Then practice with a partner.

1. A: _____*Is*_____ your signature on the check?

   B: Yes, it _____.

2. A: _____ the library open in the evening?

   B: Yes, it _____.

3. A: _____ the bank on State Street?

   B: No, it _____.

4. A: _____ I near the bank?

   B: Yes, you _____.

INFORMATION QUESTIONS WITH *BE*

						Contractions
What	**is**	your name?	What	**are**	your hours?	What's
Where	**is**	the supermarket?	Where	**are**	your books?	Where's
When	**is**	the next holiday?	When	**are**	banks open?	When's
Who	**is**	your teacher?	Who	**are**	Mutt and Jeff?	Who's
How much	**is**	one notebook?	How much	**are**	the notebooks?	

3 Match the questions and answers.

1. _e_ What is on your chair?
2. ___ Who is your doctor?
3. ___ When is the post office closed?
4. ___ How much is a notebook?
5. ___ Who are Bob, John, and Tina?
6. ___ Where are the videos?
7. ___ How much are the magazines?

a. They are my classmates.

b. It's about $3.00.

c. They're on my desk.

d. Dr. Baldwin

e. my book and my notebook

f. on Sunday

g. They are $5.00.

4 Complete the conversations. Then practice with a partner.

1. A: _____*When's*_____ the post office open on Saturday?

   B: It's open from 9 to noon.

2. A: _____ the man on the one dollar bill?

   B: He's George Washington.

3. A: _____ the chairs?

   B: They're in Room 102.

4. A: _____ the bus stop?

   B: It's across the street.

5. A: _____ ten plus ten?

   B: It's twenty.

6. A: _____ the U.S. President?

   B: _____.

LESSON 1

When is your birthday?

① _____

② _____

1 Learn New Words 🎧

Look at the pictures. Listen to the words. Then listen and repeat.

① January	⑦ July	⑬ cold
② February	⑧ August	⑭ warm
③ March	⑨ September	⑮ hot
④ April	⑩ October	⑯ rainy
⑤ May	⑪ November	⑰ sunny
⑥ June	⑫ December	⑱ cloudy

Write the words under the pictures.

⑦ _____   ⑧ _____

2 Write

Complete the sentences. Then read your sentences to a partner.

1. We are now in the month of _____.
2. It's hot here in _____.
3. It's cold here in _____.
4. It's rainy here in _____.
5. My birthday is in _____.
6. My favorite month is _____.
7. Next month is _____.

Weather Words

⑬ _____

3 Interview

Interview 5 classmates. Write their answers in a chart like this.

EXAMPLE: A: When is your birthday?
          B: It's in September.

NAME	WHEN IS YOUR BIRTHDAY?
Mei	September
_____	_____

How many birthdays are in each month?

⑮ _____

⑰ _____

Months of the Year

(3) _____

(4) _____

(5) _____

(6) _____

(9) _____

(10) _____

(11) _____

(12) _____

(14) _____

(16) _____

(18) _____

WINDOW ON GRAMMAR
Questions with *How many*

A Read the questions.

> **How many** month**s** are in a year?
> **How many** week**s** are in a year?
> **How many** day**s** are in a year?

B Complete the questions. (Many answers are possible.) Then ask a partner.

| months | weeks | days | hours | minutes |

1. How many _____ are in a week?
2. How many _____ are in a day?
3. How many _____ are in an hour?
4. How many _____ are in February?
5. How many _____ are in August?

LESSON 2

The party is on Sunday.

Sunday	Mon

THINGS TO DO

1 Learn Ordinal Numbers 🎧

Listen to the numbers. Then listen and repeat.

1st first	2nd second	3rd third	4th fourth
5th fifth	6th sixth	7th seventh	8th eighth
9th ninth	10th tenth	11th eleventh	12th twelfth
13th thirteenth	14th fourteenth	15th fifteenth	16th sixteenth

2 Learn New Words 🎧

Look at the pictures. Listen to the words. Then listen and repeat.

1. doctor's appointment
2. computer class
3. birthday party
4. PTO meeting
5. job interview
6. basketball game
7. dentist's appointment

Work with a partner. Ask about Alice. Ask about each picture.

A: When is Alice's doctor's appointment ?

B: It's on May first .

A: What day is that?

B: Tuesday .

3 Practice the Conversation 🎧

Listen to the conversation. Then listen and repeat.

A: Alice, do you want to meet on the first ?

B: What day is that?

A: Tuesday .

B: Oh, sorry. I have a doctor's appointment on the first .

Practice the conversation with a partner. Ask about these dates.

1. third
2. sixth
3. eighth
4. ninth
5. 💡

54

MAY

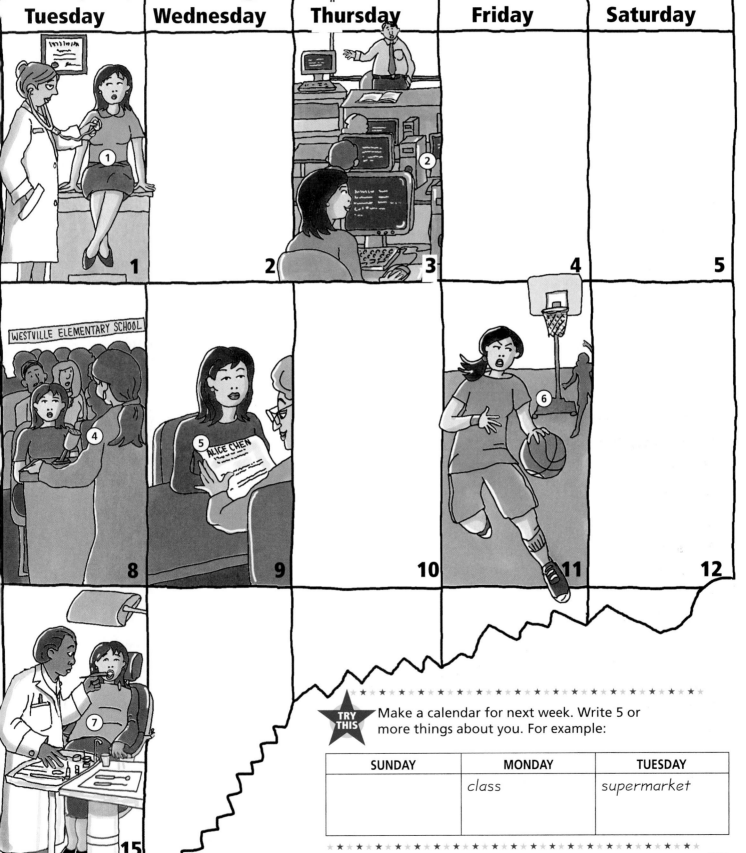

Make a calendar for next week. Write 5 or more things about you. For example:

SUNDAY	MONDAY	TUESDAY
	class	supermarket

3 LESSON

What's the date?

THINGS TO DO

1 Learn Ordinal Numbers 🎧

Listen to the numbers. Then listen and repeat.

17th seventeenth	18th eighteenth	19th nineteenth	20th twentieth
21st twenty-first	22nd twenty-second	23rd twenty-third	24th twenty-fourth
25th twenty-fifth	26th twenty-sixth	27th twenty-seventh	28th twenty-eighth

2 Write

Complete the chart. Use the appointment cards and calendar.

Name	Date	Time	Day
Henry	June 22	10 A.M.	Friday
Sue			
Nancy			
Alice			
Sam			

3 Practice the Conversation 🎧

Listen to the conversation. Then listen and repeat.

A: When's Henry's appointment?

B: It's on June twenty-second .

A: What time?

B: At 10:00 A.M.

A: What day is that?

B: Friday .

Practice the conversation with a partner. Ask about these people.

 Sue's   Nancy's   Alice's   Paul's   Lisa's

Sue Chen

has an appointment on

(M) TU W TH F

June 18 @ _4 p.m._

Please call to cancel.

Henry Chen

HAS AN APPOINTMENT ON

June 22 AT _10 a.m._

If Unable To Keep Appointment Kindly Give 24 Hours N

 Randolph Optomet

Next appointment for:

Lisa Chen

Date: _June 20_   Time: _4 p.m._

Mon.   Tues.   (Wed.)
Thurs.   Fri.

DENTAL ASSOCIATES OF CENTRAL NEW YORK

Appointment Card

For: _Chris Chen_

On: _June 25_

At: _9 a.m._

M ✓
T ___
W ___
TH ___
F ___

If unable to keep this appointment, kindly give 24 hours notice.

Nancy Chen

has an appointment on

June 27 @ 12 p.m.

M   TU   (W)   TH   F

*Please kindly give us 24 hours notice if you will
need to cancel your appointment. Thank you!*

Appointment Card

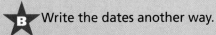

Alice Chen

June 28 @ 11 a.m.

Mon.   Tues.   Wed.   (Thurs.)   Fri.

Name: Sam Chen

Your next appointment is on:

June 21 at 9 a.m.

*We reserve the right to charge for appointments canceled
or broken without 24 hours advance notice.*

Name: Paul Chen

Your next appointment is on:

June 19 at 9 a.m.

Mon.   <u>Tues.</u>   Wed.   Thurs.   Fri.

JUNE

SUN	MON	TUE	WED	THU	FRI	SAT
					1	2
3	4	5	6	7	8	9
10	11	12	13	14	15	16
17	18	19	20	21	22	23
24	25	26	27	28	29	30

WINDOW ON MATH
Writing Dates

A Read these dates.

> 12/25/02 = December 25, 2002
> 1/1/95 = January 1, 1995
> 8/19/03 = August 19, 2003

B Write the dates another way.

3/16/80 = _____   April 11, 1944 = _____

5/19/01 = _____   February 17, 2002 = _____

C What's the date today? Write it 2 ways.

_____   _____

57

LESSON 4

Holidays

THINGS TO DO

1 Read 🎧

Read about 6 holidays in the United States. Take notes in the chart. Share your answers with a partner.

NAME OF HOLIDAY	WHEN?
1. New Year's Day	January 1
2.	
3.	
4.	
5.	
6.	

2 Write

Answer the questions.

WHAT'S YOUR FAVORITE HOLIDAY?	WHEN IS IT?

3 Interview

Ask 5 classmates about their favorite holidays. Make a chart like this. Write their answers.

A: What's your favorite holiday?

B: New Year's Day .

A: When is it?

B: In January .

NAME	HOLIDAY	MONTH
Jaime	New Year's Day	January

For people in the United States, New Year's Day is on January 1. That's the first day of the new year.

Election Day in the United States is on the first Tuesday after the first Monday in November.

Valentine's Day is on February 14.

In the United States, Independence Day is on the fourth of July.

Labor Day is on the first Monday in September. This holiday is for workers in the United States.

Thanksgiving is a big holiday in the United States. It's on the fourth Thursday in November.

WINDOW ON GRAMMAR
Singular and Plural Nouns

A Read the words.

SINGULAR		PLURAL	SINGULAR		PLURAL
holid**ay**	–	holiday**s**	fami**ly**	–	famil**ies**
ban**k**	–	bank**s**	libra**ry**	–	librar**ies**
mon**th**	–	month**s**	count**ry**	–	countr**ies**
minut**e**	–	minute**s**	par**ty**	–	part**ies**

B Write the missing singular or plural form.

one family/two _____

one school/two _____

one city/two _____

one _____/two states

one _____/two hours

one _____/two post offices

LESSON 5

I need to cancel my appointment.

1 Practice the Conversation: Making an Appointment

Listen to the conversation. Then listen and repeat.

A: Dr. Lambert's office.

B: Yes, this is Jim Brown . I'd like to make an appointment.

A: Okay. Our next opening is on March 6th at 11:00 .

B: Great. I'll take it.

Practice the conversation with a partner.
Use these items.

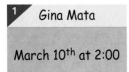
1
Gina Mata

March 10th at 2:00

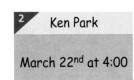
2
Ken Park

March 22nd at 4:00

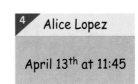
3
Tom Lin

April 12th at 10:30

4
Alice Lopez

April 13th at 11:45

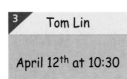
5

2 Practice the Conversation: Canceling an Appointment

Listen to the conversation. Then listen and repeat.

A: Dr. Lambert's office.

B: This is Jim Brown . I need to cancel my appointment.

A: When is it?

B: It's on March 6th at 11:00 .

A: Okay. Thanks for calling.

Practice the conversation with a partner.
Use these items.

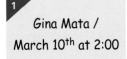
1
Gina Mata /
March 10th at 2:00

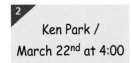
2
Ken Park /
March 22nd at 4:00

3
Tom Lin /
April 12th at 10:30

4
Alice Lopez /
April 13th at 11:45

5

3 Practice the Conversation: Rescheduling an Appointment

Listen to the conversation. Then listen and repeat.

A: Dr. Lambert's office.

B: This is Jim Brown . I need to reschedule my appointment.

A: Okay. I have an opening on May 5th at 2:00 .

B: That's good. Thank you.

Practice the conversation with a partner.
Use these items.

1 Gina Mata	2 Ken Park	3 Tom Lin	4 Alice Lopez	5
May 12th at 5:00	May 16th at 3:00	April 28th at 4:15	September 20th at 8:00	

WINDOW ON PRONUNCIATION 🎧
Short *A* and Long *A*

 A Listen to the words. Then listen and repeat.

1. male	5. make	9. map	13. raise	17. state
2. gas	6. magazine	10. back	14. after	18. day
3. date	7. basketball	11. May	15. table	19. April
4. that	8. cashier	12. rainy	16. okay	20. sale

Write the words in the correct place.

Sounds like letter *A* (long *A*)	Sounds like *a* in map (short *A*)
male, date	*gas, that*

B Work with a partner. Ask and answer the questions.

1. Is Texas a city or a state?
2. What date is today?
3. What month is after April?
4. What days of the week is your class?
5. Is Saturday before or after Friday?

School Calendars

1 Read

Read the school calendar. Answer the questions below.

SOUTH BEACH CITY PUBLIC SCHOOLS

First Semester

September 2 (Mon.)	Labor Day (Holiday – Schools Closed)
September 3 (Tues.)	First Day of School
October 4 (Fri.)	Progress Reports Issued
November 11 (Mon.)	Veterans' Day (Holiday – Schools Closed)
November 12 (Tues.)	Progress Reports Issued
November 28 and 29 (Thurs., Fri.)	Thanksgiving (Holiday – Schools Closed)
December 11 (Wed.)	Report Cards Issued
December 23 – January 1	Winter Holidays (Schools Closed)

PROGRESS REPORT

SOUTH BEACH CITY JR. HIGH SCHOOL

Grade: 07
Year: 2004-05

Student Name: Dita Warner
Student ID: 6072

Course	Number	Teacher	Term 1	Term 2
English	112	Gallo, F	S	S
World Civics	211	Truncelino, E	N	S
Earth Science	311	Bennet, H	S	S
Geometry	421	Tedone, A	S	S
German	622	Gebhart, E	N	N
	350	Langdon, J	S	S

1. When is the first day of school in South Beach?

   _____

2. What holiday is in September?

   _____

3. When are the schools closed in November?

   _____

4. How many holidays are there between September 1 and December 1?

   _____

5. When are Progress Reports issued?

   _____

6. When do you think school opens after the Winter Holidays?

   _____

REPORT CARD

SOUTH BEACH CITY JR. HIGH SCHOOL

Grade: 07
Year: 2004-05

Student Name: Brian Teese
Student ID: 7470

Course	Number	Teacher	Term 1	Term 2
English	112	Mearek, S	98	97
World Civics	211	Colman, D	82	86
Earth Science	311	Bennet, H	83	89
Geometry	421	Tambrey, J	95	94
Italian	722	Fabriano, C	72	81
Phys Ed	350	Langdon, J	93	95

Absences: 3
Tardy: 0

2 Mark the Calendar

Write the South Beach school events and holidays on the calendar for November.

NOVEMBER

SUN	MON	TUE	WED	THU	FRI	SAT
					1	2
3	4	5	6	7	8	9
10	11	12 *Progress Reports issued*	13	14	15	16
17	18	19	20	21	22	23
24	25	26	27	28	29	30

3 Write

Make a calendar for next month. Write the name of the month. Write the dates.
Write important events on your calendar.

Month : _____

SUN	MON	TUE	WED	THU	FRI	SAT

UNIT 4: Calendars

What do you know?

LESSON 7

1 Listening Review 🎧

Listen and choose the word you hear. Use the Answer Sheet.

1. A. country   B. countries
2. A. month   B. months
3. A. holiday   B. holidays
4. A. family   B. families

5. A. dollar   B. dollars
6. A. cent   B. cents
7. A. state   B. states
8. A. city   B. cities

Listen and choose the best answer. Use the Answer Sheet.

9. A. on Monday
   B. at 5
   C. 7

10. A. twelve
    B. January
    C. December

11. A. February
    B. the eighth
    C. Monday

12. A. Sunday
    B. Tuesday
    C. Thursday

13. A. August
    B. October
    C. November

14. A. in Mexico
    B. in November
    C. in the city

ANSWER SHEET

1	A	B	
2	A	B	
3	A	B	
4	A	B	
5	A	B	
6	A	B	
7	A	B	
8	A	B	
9	A	B	C
10	A	B	C
11	A	B	C
12	A	B	C
13	A	B	C
14	A	B	C
15	A	B	C
16	A	B	C

Listen and choose the correct appointment card. Use the Answer Sheet.

15.

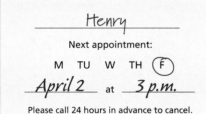

A.

Henry
Next appointment:
M TU W TH Ⓕ
April 2 at 3 p.m.
Please call 24 hours in advance to cancel.

B.

Appointment
Paul
April 12 @ 3 p.m.
☐Mon. ☐Tues. ☑Wed. ☐Thurs. ☐Fri.

C.

Jon's
appointment
April 22 at 3 p.m.
MON TUE WED ⓉHU FRI SAT

16.

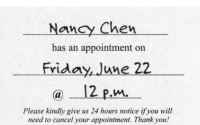

A.

Nancy Chen
has an appointment on
Friday, June 22
@ 12 p.m.
Please kindly give us 24 hours notice if you will
need to cancel your appointment. Thank you!

B.

Name: Sam
Your next appointment is on:
Monday, May 19
at 9 a.m.
If Unable To Keep Appointment Kindly Give 24 Hours Notice.

C.

APPOINTMENT
Sue
June 20 at 2 p.m.
☐MON. ☐TUES. ☑WED. ☐THURS. ☐FRI.

64

2 Conversation Check: Pair Work

Student A: Go to page 165.

Student B: Ask your partner questions about appointment
cards 1 and 2. Answer questions about cards 3 and 4.

EXAMPLE: **B:** When is John's appointment?
A: It's on March 9.
B: What time?

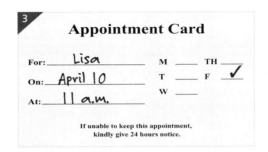

1

John

Has an appointment on:

March 9 at _____

Mon.   Tues.   Wed.   Thurs.   Fri.

2

Name: Sue

Your next appointment is on:

_____ at _____

*We reserve the right to charge for appointments canceled
or broken without 24 hours advance notice.*

3   **Appointment Card**

For: Lisa   M ____   TH ____ ✓

On: April 10   T ____   F ____

At: 11 a.m.   W ____

*If unable to keep this appointment,
kindly give 24 hours notice.*

4   ***Appointment***

For: Paul

July 8 @ 2 p.m.

☑ Mon. ☐ Tues. ☐ Wed. ☐ Thurs. ☐ Fri.

	How many questions did you ask your partner?	How many questions did you answer?
✓	☐ 1 ☐ 2 ☐ 3 ☐ 4 ☐ 5	☐ 1 ☐ 2 ☐ 3 ☐ 4 ☐ 5

✓ LEARNING LOG

I know these words:

- ☐ appointment
- ☐ April
- ☐ August
- ☐ basketball game
- ☐ birthday party
- ☐ cloudy
- ☐ cold
- ☐ December
- ☐ dentist's appointment
- ☐ doctor's appointment

- ☐ eighteenth
- ☐ eighth
- ☐ eleventh
- ☐ February
- ☐ fifteenth
- ☐ fifth
- ☐ first
- ☐ fourteenth
- ☐ fourth
- ☐ hot

- ☐ January
- ☐ job interview
- ☐ July
- ☐ June
- ☐ March
- ☐ May
- ☐ month
- ☐ nineteenth
- ☐ ninth
- ☐ November

- ☐ October
- ☐ PTO meeting
- ☐ rainy
- ☐ second
- ☐ September
- ☐ seventeenth
- ☐ seventh
- ☐ sixteenth
- ☐ sixth
- ☐ sunny

- ☐ tenth
- ☐ third
- ☐ thirteenth
- ☐ thirtieth
- ☐ twelfth
- ☐ twentieth
- ☐ warm
- ☐ weather

I can ask:

- ☐ When is your birthday?
- ☐ What day is that?
- ☐ When is your appointment?
- ☐ When is Labor Day?

I can say:

- ☐ It's on May first.
- ☐ I'd like to make an appointment.
- ☐ I need to cancel an appointment.
- ☐ I'd like to reschedule my appointment.

I can write:

- ☐ dates in two ways
- ☐ appointments on a calendar

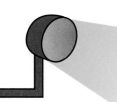

Spotlight: Writing

1 Read stories A and B below. Find these words.

Find the singular nouns with these letters.

h <u>o</u> <u>l</u> <u>i</u> <u>d</u> <u>a</u> <u>y</u>

m __ __ __ __ __

f __ __ __ __ __

f __ __ __ __ __

c __ __ __ __ __ __

Find the plural nouns.

__ __ __ __ __ __ s

__ __ __ __ __ __ __ __ s

__ __ __ __ __ __ __ s

__ __ __ __ __ __ __ s

Stories 🎧

A.

My name in Ling. My favorite holiday is Chinese New Year. It's in January or February. I like this holiday because I get money from my mother and father. We go to see the parades. We watch the fireworks at night and eat a lot of food, too.

B.

My name is Eduardo. My favorite holiday is Christmas. It's in December. I like this holiday because I am with my family. We go to church. We go to parties and give presents.

2 Correct the punctuation. Add 10 capital letters.

my name is fatima. my favorite holiday is ramadan. this year it is in march. i like this holiday because i visit with my family. we go to egypt to see them.

FOCUS ON WRITING: Capital Letters

Capitalize:

- the first word in a sentence.
  EXAMPLE: He is a doctor.
- a person's first and last name.
  EXAMPLE: John Smith
- the name of a country, state, or city.
  EXAMPLE: Mexico, California, Los Angeles
- the name of a language.
  EXAMPLE: English, Spanish, Chinese
- the days of the week.
  EXAMPLE: Monday
- the months of the year.
  EXAMPLE: January
- the name of a holiday.
  EXAMPLE: Thanksgiving
- the pronoun *I*.
  EXAMPLE: This is where I live.

3 Write your own story.

My name is _____.

_____

_____

_____

_____

_____

_____

_____

_____

Add your picture here.

LESSON 1

Shirts, Skirts, and Sweaters

Clothes for M

THINGS TO DO

1 Learn New Words 🎧

Look at the pictures. Listen to the words. Then listen and repeat.

① necktie	⑦ shirt	⑬ socks
② undershirt	⑧ sweater	⑭ pants
③ briefs	⑨ hat	⑮ shorts
④ shoes	⑩ T-shirt	⑯ blouse
⑤ boots	⑪ jacket	⑰ skirt
⑥ coat	⑫ pajamas	⑱ dress

Write the words above the pictures.

2 Learn New Words 🎧

Look at the squares. Listen to the colors. Then listen and repeat.

blue	yellow	red	black
brown	green	purple	white

3 Practice the Conversation 🎧

Listen to the conversation. Then listen and repeat.

A: What color is the jacket ?

B: It's brown .

Practice the conversation with a partner. Use these items from the pictures.

1 coat	2 skirt	3 T-shirt	4 necktie	5 💡

① _____

⑥ _____

② _____

⑩ _____

③ _____

TRY THIS

Choose 3 colors and make a chart. List 5 thi in your classroom for each color.

blue	white	yellow
Ann's sweater	Juan's shirt	my noteboo

Clothes for Men and Women

Clothes for Women

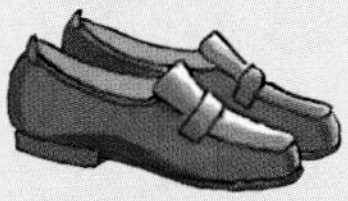

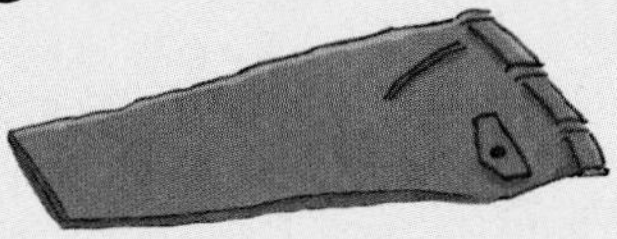

④ _____

⑤ _____

⑯ _____

⑦ _____

⑧ _____

⑨ _____

⑰ _____

⑬ _____

⑪ _____

⑫ _____

⑱ _____

⑭ _____

⑮ _____

WINDOW ON GRAMMAR
Present Continuous Statements

A Read the sentences.

> I **am wearing** a blue jacket.
> They **are wearing** red shoes.
> My friend **is wearing** black pants.

B Complete the sentences.

1. I _____ wearing _____ .

2. The person next to me _____ wearing

_____ .

3. Three people in the room _____ wearing

_____ .

LESSON 2

I'm looking for children's clothes.

THINGS TO DO

1 Learn New Words 🎧

Look at the picture. Listen to the words. Then listen and repeat.

PEOPLE AND PLACES

1. department store
2. fitting room
3. customer
4. customer service
5. cashier
6. exit
7. entrance

ACTIONS

8. coming into
9. going into
10. talking
11. sleeping
12. leaving
13. running
14. buying

2 Practice the Conversation 🎧

Listen to the conversation. Then listen and repeat.

A: Where's Marc ?
B: He's near the exit .
A: What's he doing?
B: He's leaving the store .

Practice the conversation with a partner. Ask about these people.

1	2	3	4
Sam	Sara	Tom	Ed

3 Practice the Conversation 🎧

Listen to the conversation. Then listen and repeat.

A: Can I help you?
B: Yes, I'm looking for children's clothes .
A: They're on the second floor.
B: Thank you.

Practice the conversation with a partner. Ask about the places in the store directory.

STORE DIRECTORY

Children's Clothes	2nd floor
Children's Shoes	3rd floor
Women's Clothes	1st floor
Women's Coats	4th floor
Women's Shoes	3rd floor
Men's Clothes	1st floor
Men's Coats	4th floor
Men's Shoes	2nd floor
Sleepwear	3rd floor

STORE DIRECTORY

Children's Clothes 2⁰ floor
Children's Clothes 3⁰ floor
Women's Shoes 3⁰ floor
Men's Clothes 1⁰ floor
Men's Coats floor

Ed and Don

SCARVES

UNIT 5: Clothing

What size is it?

LESSON 3

THINGS TO DO

1 Learn New Words

Look at the pictures. Listen to the words. Then listen and repeat.

① price tag ③ size ⑤ medium ⑦ extra large
② receipt ④ small ⑥ large

2 Practice the Conversation

Listen to the conversation. Then listen and repeat.

A: What size is the T-shirt ?
B: It's a small .
A: Really? Is it on sale?
B: Yes. It's only five dollars .
A: Wow! Five dollars ! That's a good price.

Practice the conversation with a partner. Ask about these items.

| 1 sweater | 2 blouse | 3 coat | 4 jacket | 5 dress |

★ ★

 TRY THIS   Buy 3 things from Lane's Department Store.
Write the store receipt.

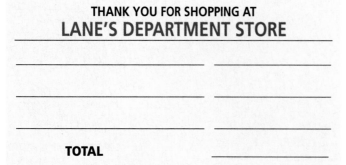

THANK YOU FOR SHOPPING AT
LANE'S DEPARTMENT STORE

_____ _____

_____ _____

_____ _____

TOTAL _____

★ ★

SALE
Lane's Department Store

SIZE: MEDIUM
$10.00
PRICE: $20.00

SIZE: EXTRA LARGE
$15.00
PRICE: $30.00

SIZE: LARGE
$30.00
PRICE: $60.00

THANK YOU FOR SHOPPING AT
LANE'S DEPARTMENT STORE

	$5.00
T-shirt	$10.00
Blouse	$30.00
Coat	$15.00
Sweater	$25.00
Jacket	$20.00
Dress	
SUB-TOTAL	$105.00
TAX	$5.25
TOTAL	$110.25

WINDOW ON MATH 🎧
Multiplying and Dividing

A Listen to the sentences. Then listen and repeat.

1. Six times two equals twelve. ($6 \times 2 = 12$)
2. Twelve times two equals twenty-four. ($12 \times 2 = 24$)
3. Six divided by two equals three. ($6 \div 2 = 3$)
4. Twelve divided by two equals six. ($12 \div 2 = 6$)

B Write the missing words.

1. Ten _____ two equals twenty.
2. Six _____ one equals six.
3. Four _____ by two equals two.
4. Four _____ four equals sixteen.
5. _____ times _____ equals _____.
6. _____ divided by _____ equals _____.

73

★ A Folktale

LESSON 4

THINGS TO DO

1 Learn New Words 🎧

Look at the pictures. Listen to the words. Then listen and repeat.

① big hole
② cutting
③ scissors
④ tailor

2 Read 🎧

Look at the pictures. Listen to the story. Then complete the story chart.

STORY CHART

At the beginning of the story, Leo is wearing _____ .

⬇

Next, Leo is wearing _____ .

⬇

Five years later Leo is wearing _____ .

3 Predict 🎧

What is the missing word at the end of the story? Share ideas with your classmates. Then listen and compare.

At the end of the story, Leo is wearing ___**?**___ .

This is a story about Simon and Leo. Simon is a tailor. Leo is his friend. One day Leo comes into Simon's store. Leo is wearing a very old coat.

LEO: Oh, Simon, there is a big hole in my coat. What can I do?

It is five years later.

LEO: Oh, Simon, there is a big hole in my jacket. What can I do?

Simon looks at the jacket carefully. Then he leaves the room. After an hour, he comes back.

SIMON: Here you are, Leo. Your old jacket is now a vest.

LEO: Oh, Simon, it's a beautiful vest. How can I thank you?

2

Simon looks at the coat carefully. Then he takes out his scissors.

LEO: What are you doing, Simon?

SIMON: I'm cutting up your coat.

3

Simon leaves the room with the pieces of Leo's coat. After an hour, he comes back.

SIMON: Here you are, Leo. Your old coat is now a jacket.

LEO: Oh, Simon, it's a beautiful jacket. How can I thank you?

5

It is five years later.

LEO: Oh, Simon, there is a big hole in my vest. What can I do?

Simon looks at the vest carefully. Then he leaves the room. After an hour, he comes back.

SIMON: Here you are, Leo. Your old vest is now a **?** _____.

LEO: Oh, Simon, it's beautiful. How can I thank you?

WINDOW ON GRAMMAR
Object Pronouns:
me, you, him, her, it, them, us

He is looking at <u>**me**</u>.
I am looking at <u>**you**</u>.
She is looking at <u>**him**</u>.
He is looking at <u>**her**</u>.
I am looking at <u>**it**</u>.
She is looking at <u>**them**</u>.
Our teacher is looking at <u>**us**</u>.

⭐ **A** Complete the sentences *with me, you, him, her, it, them,* or *us.*

1. Leo is talking to Simon. He is asking

   _____ a question.

2. Simon is looking at Leo's coat. He is

   looking at _____ carefully.

3. She isn't closing the windows. She is

   opening _____.

75

It's too short.

5 LESSON

1 Learn New Words 🎧

Look at the pictures. Listen to the words. Then listen and repeat.

Describe the clothes in the pictures.

1. The black skirt isn't short. It's _____.

2. The green skirt isn't too long. It's _____.

3. The brown pants aren't loose. They're _____.

4. The black pants aren't too tight. They're _____.

2 Practice the Conversation: Describing Clothes 🎧

Listen to the conversation. Then listen and repeat.

A: Do you like this dress ?

B: It's nice, but I think it's too short .

Practice the conversation with a partner. Use these items.

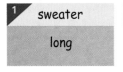 1 sweater — long

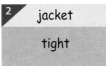 2 jacket — tight

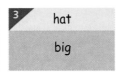 3 hat — big

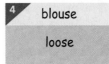 4 blouse — loose

 5

3 Practice the Conversation: Returning Something 🎧

Listen to the conversation. Then listen and repeat.

A: I'd like to return these pants .

B: What's the problem?

A: They're too short .

B: All right. No problem.

Practice the conversation with a partner.
Use these items.

1 shoes	2 pajamas	3 shorts	4 boots	5
tight	loose	tight	small	

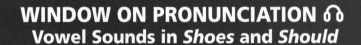

WINDOW ON PRONUNCIATION 🎧
Vowel Sounds in *Shoes* and *Should*

A Listen to the words. Then listen and repeat.

1. shoes (should) loose too
2. look book put two
3. you noon woman loose
4. boots excuse good blue

Listen again. Circle the word that has a different vowel sound.

B Listen to the words. Then listen and repeat.

1. blue   a. book
2. good   b. June
3. cook   c. shoe
4. noon   d. should

Work with a partner. Match the words that have the same sound.

77

Work Clothes

1 Ask Questions

Work with a partner. Ask and answer questions about clothing. Use the names below.

A: What's Ken wearing?

B: He's wearing a green shirt, green pants, white shoes, and a white hat.

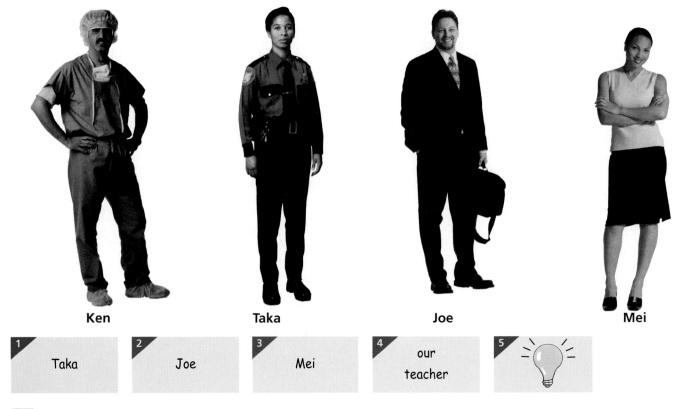

| Ken | Taka | Joe | Mei |

| 1 Taka | 2 Joe | 3 Mei | 4 our teacher | 5 |

2 Give Opinions

Work with a partner. Match Ken, Taka, Joe, and Mei to his or her occupation.

Occupations			
dentist	bus driver	teacher	nurse
librarian	police officer	pharmacist	cashier

A: What's Ken's occupation?

B: I think he is a _____.

A: Why?

B: Because he's wearing _____.

3 Read

Read the memo. Then complete the sentences about Leila, Phil, and Rob.

Smith Industries

Memo

To: All Employees
Topic: Work Clothes

From: Louis Smith
Date: August 1, 2004

All employees should dress appropriately. If your clothes are not appropriate, your supervisor may ask you to go home.

Inappropriate Work Clothes					
jeans		shorts or short skirts		baseball caps	
T-shirts		sneakers		sandals	

Leila

Leila's clothes are inappropriate for work because she is wearing

_____
_____
_____.

Phil

Phil's clothes are inappropriate for work because he is wearing

_____
_____
_____.

Rob

Rob's clothes are inappropriate for work because he is wearing

_____
_____
_____.

7 LESSON

What do you know?

1 Listening Review 🎧

Listen and choose the correct answer. Use the Answer Sheet.

1. A. medium
   B. $15.00
   C. blue

2. A. a sweater
   B. brown
   C. at the department store

3. A. on the 2nd floor
   B. He's leaving.
   C. pajamas

4. A. red
   B. on sale
   C. a small

5. A. It's nice.
   B. Yes, it is.
   C. Thanks.

6. A. It's extra large.
   B. It's blue.
   C. fifty dollars

7. A. It's a green sweater.
   B. They're next to the elevator.
   C. They're too small.

8. A. Yes, it is.
   B. Yes, they are.
   C. Yes, there are.

ANSWER SHEET

1	Ⓐ	Ⓑ	Ⓒ
2	Ⓐ	Ⓑ	Ⓒ
3	Ⓐ	Ⓑ	Ⓒ
4	Ⓐ	Ⓑ	Ⓒ
5	Ⓐ	Ⓑ	Ⓒ
6	Ⓐ	Ⓑ	Ⓒ
7	Ⓐ	Ⓑ	Ⓒ
8	Ⓐ	Ⓑ	Ⓒ

2 Dictation 🎧

Listen and write the questions you hear.

1. _____

   _____

2. _____

   _____

3. _____

   _____

Work with a partner. Ask and answer the questions.

3 Conversation Check: Pair Work

Student A: Go to page 166.

Student B: Ask your partner questions to complete the price tags.

EXAMPLE: B: What size is the blue sweater?
A: It's an extra large.
B: How much is it?

a. Size: LARGE Price: $40.00
b. Size: Extra Large Price:
c. Size: SMALL Price: $25.00
d. Size: Price:

How many questions did you ask your partner?	How many questions did you answer?
☐ 1 ☐ 2 ☐ 3 ☐ 4	☐ 1 ☐ 2 ☐ 3 ☐ 4

✔ LEARNING LOG

I know these words:

☐ big	☐ cutting	☐ jacket	☐ purple	☐ sock
☐ black	☐ department	☐ large	☐ receipt	☐ sweater
☐ blouse	store	☐ leaving	☐ red	☐ tailor
☐ blue	☐ divided by	☐ long	☐ running	☐ talking to
☐ boot	☐ dress	☐ looking for	☐ scissors	☐ tight
☐ briefs	☐ entrance	☐ loose	☐ shirt	☐ times
☐ brown	☐ exit	☐ medium	☐ shoe	☐ too
☐ buying	☐ extra large	☐ men	☐ short	☐ T-shirt
☐ cap	☐ fitting room	☐ necktie	☐ shorts	☐ undershirt
☐ coat	☐ going into	☐ pajamas	☐ size	☐ wearing
☐ coming into	☐ green	☐ pants	☐ skirt	☐ white
☐ customer	☐ hat	☐ price	☐ sleeping	☐ women
☐ customer service	☐ hole	☐ price tag	☐ small	☐ yellow

I can ask:

☐ What color is the jacket?
☐ What's he doing?
☐ What size is the shirt?
☐ Do you like this dress?
☐ What's the problem?
☐ What's her occupation?

I can say:

☐ I'm looking for children's clothes.
☐ He's wearing a coat.
☐ It's too short.
☐ I'd like to return these pants.
☐ $6 \times 2 = 12$
☐ $12 \div 2 = 6$

I can write:

☐ a store receipt

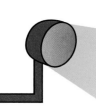

Spotlight: Grammar

PRESENT CONTINUOUS		
I	am am not	
You We They	are are not	working.
He She It	is is not	

1 Write *am, is,* or *are.*

1. Louis ____is____ reading in the library.

2. Tom and Tina _____ talking on the telephone.

3. Erik _____ wearing his new jacket.

4. I _____ reading a book.

5. You and I _____ sitting in class.

6. I _____ doing my homework.

7. We _____ eating lunch.

8. She _____ sitting at her desk.

2 Write about the people in the pictures.

1.  *They are running.*

2. _____

3.  _____

4. _____

5. _____

6.  _____

INFORMATION QUESTIONS WITH THE PRESENT CONTINUOUS

What	is	she reading?	What	are	you reading?
Where	is	he sitting?	Where	are	they sitting?
Why	is	Mr. Smith leaving?	Why	are	Mr. and Mrs. Smith leaving?
Who	is	sitting down?	Who	are	you talking to?

3 Match the questions and answers.

1. __d__ What is he doing?
2. _____ Where is she reading?
3. _____ Who are you talking to?
4. _____ Why are you wearing shorts?
5. _____ What are you watching?

a. my teacher
b. a movie
c. in her room
d. He's sleeping.
e. because it's hot

4 Complete the conversations. Then practice with a partner.

A: _____ *What* _____ *are* _____ you reading?

B: I'm reading a library book.

A: _____ _____ she wearing?

B: She's wearing a blue dress.

A: _____ _____ they going?

B: They're going to Lane's Department Store.

A: _____ _____ you listening to?

B: We're listening to the radio.

A: _____ is sitting next to you?

B: _____

A: _____ are you sitting next to?

B: _____

LESSON 1

Noodles are delicious.

THINGS TO DO

1 Learn New Words 🎧

Look at the pictures. Listen to the words. Then listen and repeat.

① noodles	⑧ bananas	⑮ shrimp
② bread	⑨ milk	⑯ beans
③ rice	⑩ cheese	⑰ onions
④ cereal	⑪ yogurt	⑱ tomatoes
⑤ apples	⑫ butter	⑲ lettuce
⑥ oranges	⑬ peanuts	⑳ carrots
⑦ grapes	⑭ chicken	

Write the words next to the pictures. Then add another food to each group.

2 Give Opinions

Group the foods above. Put the words that end in *-s* in Group 1. Put the other words into Group 2.

GROUP 1	GROUP 2
noodles	bread

Work with a partner. Give your opinion of 5 foods.

I think noodles <u>are</u> delicious.

I think bread <u>is</u> good.

delicious   good   terrible

3 Write

Make a shopping list like this. Write 10 foods.

SHOPPING LIST	
Fruit & Vegetables	Dairy
apples	milk
Grains	Other
bread	

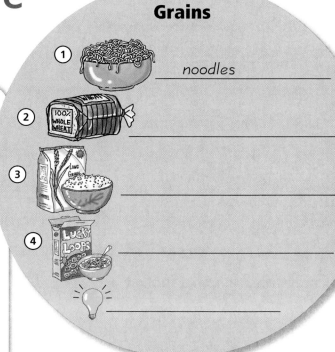

Grains

① _noodles_

②

③

④

⊢ **FOOD**

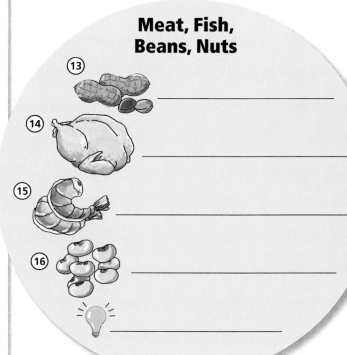

Meat, Fish, Beans, Nuts

⑬

⑭

⑮

⑯

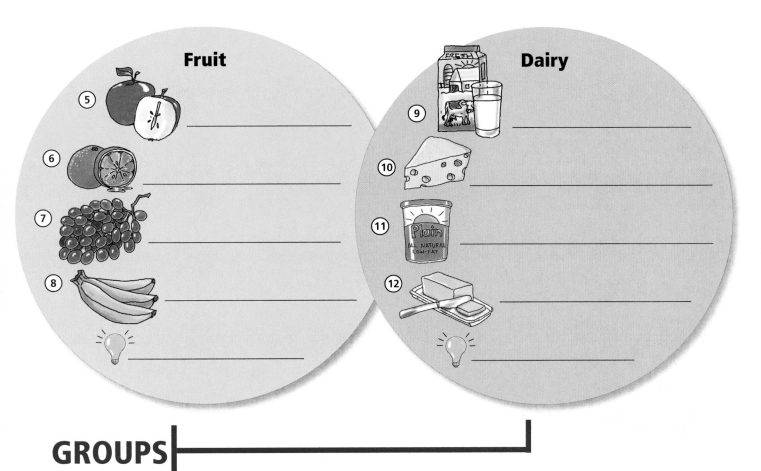

Fruit

5 _____

6 _____

7 _____

8 _____

💡 _____

Dairy

9 _____

10 _____

11 _____

12 _____

💡 _____

GROUPS

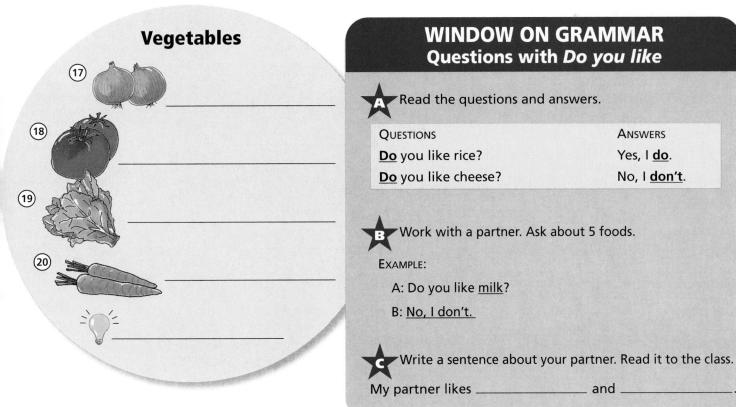

Vegetables

17 _____

18 _____

19 _____

20 _____

💡 _____

WINDOW ON GRAMMAR
Questions with *Do you like*

⭐ **A** Read the questions and answers.

QUESTIONS	ANSWERS
Do you like rice?	Yes, I **do**.
Do you like cheese?	No, I **don't**.

⭐ **B** Work with a partner. Ask about 5 foods.

EXAMPLE:

A: Do you like <u>milk</u>?

B: <u>No, I don't.</u>

⭐ **C** Write a sentence about your partner. Read it to the class.

My partner likes _____ and _____.

2 LESSON

Do you sell rice?

THINGS TO DO

1 Talk About the Picture

Write 5 things about the picture.

> EXAMPLES: Gail is looking at paper towels.
> Tina is standing in line.

Share your ideas with the class.

2 Learn New Words 🎧

Look at the picture. Listen to the words. Then listen and repeat.

① Aisle 1
② restroom
③ ice
④ frozen foods
⑤ produce section

⑥ shopping cart
⑦ mop
⑧ checkout counter
⑨ coupons
⑩ bakery

⑪ pushing a cart
⑫ looking at
⑬ eating
⑭ cleaning the floor
⑮ standing in line

3 Practice the Conversation 🎧

Listen to the conversations. Then listen and repeat.

A: Excuse me. Do you sell rice ?
B: Yes, we do. It's in Aisle 1 .
A: Thank you.
B: You're welcome.

A: Excuse me. Do you sell bananas ?
B: Yes, we do. They're in the produce section .
A: Thank you.
B: You're welcome.

Practice the conversations with a partner. Ask about these things.

3 LESSON

How much is it?

THINGS TO DO

1 Learn New Words 🎧

Look at the picture. Listen to the words. Then listen and repeat.

① a bag of apples   ⑤ a jar of honey   ⑧ a bottle of oil

② a carton of milk   ⑥ a box of sugar   ⑨ expensive

③ a loaf of bread   ⑦ a can of tomatoes   ⑩ cheap

④ a package of cheese

What other foods are in the picture? Share ideas with your classmates.

2 Find Someone Who

Make a chart like this. Write 8 foods from the picture.

FOOD	PERSON'S NAME
1. a loaf of bread	Keiko
2. a jar of honey	Tina

Talk to your classmates. Find someone who has the food at home. Write the person's name.

A: Do you have a loaf of bread at home?

B: Yes, I do. / No, I don't.

3 Practice the Conversation 🎧

Listen to the conversation. Then listen and repeat.

A: Excuse me. How much is a
loaf of bread ?

B: Five dollars.

A: Wow! That's expensive.

Practice the conversation with a partner. Ask about these foods.

WINDOW ON MATH
Pounds, Ounces, and Cups

1 pound (lb.) = 16 ounces (oz.)
1 cup (c.) = 8 fluid ounces (oz.)
16 tablespoons (tbsp) = 1 cup (c.)

 A Answer the questions.

1. How many ounces are in two pounds of shrimp?

2. How many ounces are in a pound and a half of beans?

3. You have a half cup of milk. How many ounces is that?

4. You have a half pound of lettuce. How many ounces is that?

5. You need a half cup of oil. How many tablespoons is that?

Is milk on sale?

1 Practice the Conversation: Ordering Food at a Counter 🎧

Listen to the conversation. Then listen and repeat.

A: Number 27 , please.

B: That's me.

A: What can I get for you?

B: Three pounds of chicken.

A: Anything else?

B: No, that's all.

Practice the conversation with a partner.
Use these items.

1	28	2	29	3	30	4
A pound		Half a pound		Two pounds		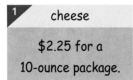

2 Practice the Conversation: Asking for Help 🎧

Listen to the conversation. Then listen and repeat.

A: Can I help you?

B: Yes. Do you have vegetable oil ?

A: Yes, we do. It's on sale this week.

B: How much is it?

A: $1.99 for a 64-ounce bottle.

Practice the conversation with a partner. Use these items.

1 cheese	2 white rice	3 bread	4
$2.25 for a 10-ounce package.	99¢ for a 16-oz. bag.	$2.50 for a 24-oz. loaf.	

3 Practice the Conversation: Asking about Sales 🎧

Listen to the conversation. Then listen and repeat.

A: Is milk on sale this week?

B: Yes. It's only 99 cents a carton .

A: What size?

B: 32 ounces.

A: Wow! That's a good price.

Practice the conversation with a partner.
Use these items.

 1 rice
a bag /
12 ounces

 2 honey
a jar /
8 ounces

 3 sugar
a box /
16 ounces

 4

WINDOW ON PRONUNCIATION 🎧
Intonation in *Yes/No* Questions

A Listen to the questions. Then listen and repeat.

1. Can I help you?

2. Do you have grape juice?

3. Is rice on sale this week?

4. Anything else?

5. Do you sell noodles?

6. Do you have a package of cheese at home?

7. Do you like apples?

Work with a partner. Ask and answer the questions.

B Listen to the sentences. Then listen and repeat.

1. A. The apples are on sale
   B. The apples are on sale

2. A. Okay
   B. Okay

3. A. Milk
   B. Milk

Listen again. Write a period after each statement and a question mark after each question.

The Food Pyramid

1 Talk About the Picture

What foods do you know in the picture below? What foods can you add to each group?

The Food Pyramid

Do you eat the right foods? This is one guide to help you choose foods that are good for you.

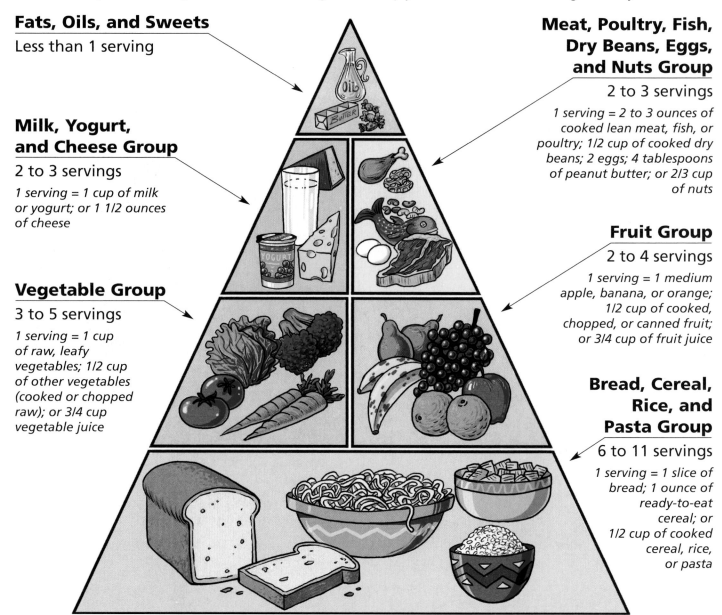

Fats, Oils, and Sweets
Less than 1 serving

Milk, Yogurt, and Cheese Group
2 to 3 servings

1 serving = 1 cup of milk or yogurt; or 1 1/2 ounces of cheese

Vegetable Group
3 to 5 servings

1 serving = 1 cup of raw, leafy vegetables; 1/2 cup of other vegetables (cooked or chopped raw); or 3/4 cup vegetable juice

Meat, Poultry, Fish, Dry Beans, Eggs, and Nuts Group
2 to 3 servings

1 serving = 2 to 3 ounces of cooked lean meat, fish, or poultry; 1/2 cup of cooked dry beans; 2 eggs; 4 tablespoons of peanut butter; or 2/3 cup of nuts

Fruit Group
2 to 4 servings

1 serving = 1 medium apple, banana, or orange; 1/2 cup of cooked, chopped, or canned fruit; or 3/4 cup of fruit juice

Bread, Cereal, Rice, and Pasta Group
6 to 11 servings

1 serving = 1 slice of bread; 1 ounce of ready-to-eat cereal; or 1/2 cup of cooked cereal, rice, or pasta

2 Read

Study the food pyramid. Complete this chart.

FOOD GROUP	NUMBER OF SERVINGS PER DAY
1. *Bread, Cereal, Rice, and Pasta Group*	*6 to 11*
2. *Fruit Group*	
3.	
4.	
5.	
6.	

3 Write

Write the number of servings.

2 slices of bread =

2 servings

4 eggs =

1½ cups of orange juice =

1 cup of cooked dry beans =

1 cup of uncooked or raw spinach =

1 cup of cooked rice =

★ ★

TRY THIS Write 4 sentences about you and people in your family.

EXAMPLES: *I eat about 5 servings of vegetables every day.*
My father always eats 1 serving of pasta at night.
I usually eat 1 serving of yogurt in the morning.
My son eats 2 servings of fruit in the evening.

★ ★

7 LESSON

What do you know?

1 Listening Review 🎧

Listen and choose the word you hear. Use the Answer Sheet.

1. A. always   B. sometimes   C. never
2. A. usually   B. sometimes   C. never
3. A. always   B. usually   C. never
4. A. always   B. sometimes   C. never

Listen and choose the best answer. Use the Answer Sheet.

5. A. Yes, I do.
   B. $5 a pound
   C. in Aisle 3

6. A. at the checkout counter
   B. Yes, we do.
   C. That's right.

7. A. It's delicious.
   B. It's $3.99.
   C. in Aisle 1

8. A. 16 ounces
   B. $1.99
   C. Yes, it is.

9. A. No, it isn't.
   B. a 12-ounce bag
   C. orange juice

10. A. That's a good price.
    B. a pound of chicken
    C. It's delicious.

ANSWER SHEET

1	Ⓐ	Ⓑ	Ⓒ
2	Ⓐ	Ⓑ	Ⓒ
3	Ⓐ	Ⓑ	Ⓒ
4	Ⓐ	Ⓑ	Ⓒ
5	Ⓐ	Ⓑ	Ⓒ
6	Ⓐ	Ⓑ	Ⓒ
7	Ⓐ	Ⓑ	Ⓒ
8	Ⓐ	Ⓑ	Ⓒ
9	Ⓐ	Ⓑ	Ⓒ
10	Ⓐ	Ⓑ	Ⓒ

2 Dictation 🎧

Listen and write the missing words.

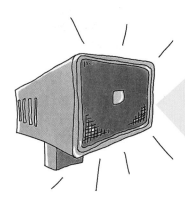

Attention, shoppers.

If you like _____ for breakfast, *Corn Crunch* is on sale today. It's

only $3.95 for a _____ box. With _____

and _____, your breakfast will be _____

and nutritious. The bananas are in the _____ section,

and the milk is in the _____ section.

3 Conversation Check: Pair Work

Student A: Go to page 166.

Student B: Ask your partner questions to complete this chart.

EXAMPLE: **B:** How much is a can of tomatoes?

A: $2.50

	FOOD	PRICE (How much?)	SIZE/AMOUNT (What size?)
1		$2.50	
2			
3		$2.00	48 ounces
4		$6.00	32 ounces

✔

How many questions did you ask your partner?	How many questions did you answer?
☐ 1 ☐ 2 ☐ 3 ☐ 4	☐ 1 ☐ 2 ☐ 3 ☐ 4

✔ LEARNING LOG

I know these words:

- ☐ aisle
- ☐ always
- ☐ apple
- ☐ bag
- ☐ bakery
- ☐ banana
- ☐ bean
- ☐ bottle
- ☐ box
- ☐ bread
- ☐ butter
- ☐ can
- ☐ carrot
- ☐ carton
- ☐ cereal

- ☐ cheap
- ☐ checkout counter
- ☐ cheese
- ☐ chicken
- ☐ clean the floor
- ☐ cooked
- ☐ coupon
- ☐ cup
- ☐ dairy
- ☐ delicious
- ☐ eat
- ☐ egg
- ☐ expensive
- ☐ fish
- ☐ food

- ☐ frozen foods
- ☐ fruit
- ☐ grain
- ☐ grape
- ☐ have
- ☐ honey
- ☐ ice
- ☐ jar
- ☐ juice
- ☐ lettuce
- ☐ like
- ☐ loaf
- ☐ look at
- ☐ meat
- ☐ milk

- ☐ mop
- ☐ never
- ☐ noodles
- ☐ nut
- ☐ oil
- ☐ onion
- ☐ on sale
- ☐ orange
- ☐ ounce
- ☐ package
- ☐ peanut
- ☐ pound
- ☐ produce section
- ☐ push a cart
- ☐ raw

- ☐ restroom
- ☐ rice
- ☐ serving
- ☐ shopping cart
- ☐ shrimp
- ☐ slice
- ☐ sometimes
- ☐ stand in line
- ☐ sugar
- ☐ terrible
- ☐ tomato
- ☐ usually
- ☐ vegetable
- ☐ yogurt

I can ask:

- ☐ Do you like noodles?
- ☐ Do you sell rice?
- ☐ How much is a loaf of bread?
- ☐ What can I get for you?
- ☐ Is milk on sale?

I can say:

- ☐ Yes, I do.
- ☐ No, I don't.
- ☐ It's 99¢.
- ☐ A pound of chicken, please.
- ☐ It's in Aisle 3.

I can write:

- ☐ food words
- ☐ sentences about a supermarket
- ☐ the price of foods
- ☐ a shopping list
- ☐ sentences about eating habits

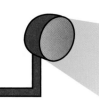

Spotlight: Writing

1 Read the recipe. Number the pictures in order from first (1) to last (5).

RECIPE

My Favorite Soup
Lucy Kimball

Ingredients

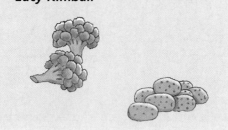

1 lb. broccoli
1 lb. potatoes
water
salt
pepper

Directions

Wash the broccoli and the potatoes. Cut the potatoes in quarters and put them in a large pot with water. Boil the potatoes for about 20 minutes. Add the broccoli and boil for 3 minutes. Put the broccoli and the potatoes into a blender. Add some of the water and blend. Add salt and pepper and serve hot.

Boil the broccoli for 3 minutes.

Wash the vegetables.

Blend the vegetables with some water.

Add salt and pepper and serve hot.

Cut up the potatoes and boil them for 20 minutes.

2 Connect the sentences. Use *and*.

1. Cook it for 30 minutes. Serve it hot.

Cook it for 30 minutes and serve it hot.

2. Put the vegetables in a blender. Blend them.

_____

_____

3. Add the broccoli. Boil it for 3 minutes.

_____

4. Cut the potatoes in quarters. Boil them.

_____

5. Put water in a large pot. Add salt.

_____

6. Cook the vegetables. Serve them hot.

_____

FOCUS ON WRITING: Connecting Sentences

Use *and* to connect two sentences.

Examples:

Cut up the potatoes. Put them in a large pot.
Cut up the potatoes **and** put them in a large pot.

Add the broccoli. Cook it for 3 minutes.
Add the broccoli **and** cook it for 3 minutes.

3 Choose a favorite recipe. Write the ingredients. Write the directions.

_____

_____

Ingredients

Directions

2
LESSON

I usually cook dinner.

THINGS TO DO

1 Learn New Words 🎧

Look at the pictures. Listen to the words. Then listen and repeat.

1. fix things
2. make the bed
3. wash the dishes
4. take out the trash
5. buy the groceries
6. pay the bills
7. clean the house
8. do the laundry
9. cook dinner

Write the words under the pictures.

2 Interview

Work with a partner. Ask the questions below. Check (✓) your partner's answers.

DO YOU _____?	YES, OFTEN.	YES, SOMETIMES.	NO, NEVER.
fix things at home	☐	☐	☐
make the beds	☐	☐	☐
wash the dishes	☐	☐	☐
take out the trash	☐	☐	☐
buy the groceries	☐	☐	☐
pay the bills	☐	☐	☐
clean the house	☐	☐	☐
do the laundry	☐	☐	☐

Share 3 things about your partner with the class.

> EXAMPLE: My partner often does the laundry.

3 Write

What do *you* do at home? Write your answer.

> EXAMPLE:
> I usually cook dinner and clean the house. I sometimes wash the dishes and take out the trash. I never pay the bills.

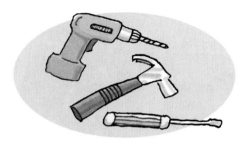

1 _____ *fix things*

9 _____

8 _____

③ _____

④ _____

Family Responsibilities

⑤ _____

⑥ _____

WINDOW ON GRAMMAR
Simple Present Statements

★**A** Read the sentences.

I **cook** dinner.	He **cooks** dinner.
You **wash** the dishes.	Jon **washes** the dishes.
We **make** the beds.	She **makes** the bed.
They **fix** things.	Ann **fixes** things.

★**B** Complete these sentences.

1. Her brother _____ the dishes on Sunday.

2. He often _____ dinner on Saturday.

3. Mei's husband always _____ the groceries.

4. Their children _____ _____ the trash.

5. Tim's parents _____ the laundry.

★**C** Write 4 sentences about people in your family.

EXAMPLE: My husband never fixes things at home.

103

3 LESSON

What do you do for fun?

THINGS TO DO

1 Talk About the Picture

Write 5 things about the picture.

EXAMPLE: The big white dog is running.

Share your ideas with the class.

2 Learn New Words 🎧

Look at the picture. Listen to the words. Then listen and repeat.

① read the newspaper   ⑤ take pictures
② play an instrument   ⑥ listen to music
③ dance   ⑦ play soccer
④ play cards   ⑧ tell stories

3 Interview

Ask your partner the questions below. Check (✓) your partner's answers.

DOES YOUR FAMILY _____?	YES, OFTEN.	YES, SOMETIMES.	NO, NEVER.
listen to music	☐	☐	☐
play cards	☐	☐	☐
play instruments	☐	☐	☐
tell stories	☐	☐	☐
play soccer	☐	☐	☐

Share 3 things about your partner with the class.

EXAMPLE: My partner's family often plays cards.

★ ★

TRY THIS Write 3 questions. Then ask a partner your questions.

Who in your family _____*plays cards*_____ ?

Who in your family _____ ?

Who in your family _____ ?

★ ★

UNIT 7: Families

Family Portraits

LESSON 4

THINGS TO DO

1 Read and Take Notes

Read about each family. Take notes in the chart below.

NAME	MARITAL STATUS	LIVES WITH
1. Pilar	married	husband and 2 children
2. Boris		
3. Sonya		
4. Nhu Trinh		

Work with a partner. Tell about each person's family.

> EXAMPLE: Pilar is married and she lives with her husband and two children.

2 Write

Write about people in your family.

1. My aunt's name is _____.

   She is my _____ sister.

2. My uncle's name is _____.

   He is my _____ brother.

3. I live with _____.

★ ★

TRY THIS Write 3 or more sentences about your family.

My name is _____.

I'm from _____. I live with

_____.

★ ★

1 My name is Pilar Garcia and I'm from Mexico. I am married and I have two children. My husband's name is Manuel. My two daughters' names are Belen and Maria. They are 12 and 14. We live together in Phoenix, and we are very happy.

4 My name is Nhu Trinh. I'm from Vietnam. I have three children. My husband and I live in California. I work at a bank in Los Angeles. My daughter and son-in-law live in Vietnam. My sons live in Arizona. I love my family, but we don't see each other very much.

106

2 My name is Boris and I'm from Russia. My wife's name is Anna. We have three children and two grandchildren. Now we live in a beautiful home with our daughter. My family is my whole life. I love my family.

3 My name is Sonya and I'm from China. I'm single. I live with my aunt and uncle. My uncle is my mother's brother. My mother and father live in China. I miss them very much.

WINDOW ON GRAMMAR
Don't and *Doesn't*

 Read the sentences.

I **don't** have children.	He **doesn't** have a sister.
We **don't** have children.	She **doesn't** have a son.
You **don't** have children.	
They **don't** have a daughter.	

 Complete these sentences with *don't* or *doesn't*.

1. I _____ have 20 children.

2. Her sister _____ have any children.

3. His parents _____ live in Canada.

4. Her children _____ live near her.

5. Their son _____ have a job.

6. My husband and I _____ live together.

★ LESSON 5

Just a minute, please.

1 Practice the Conversation: Making a Call

Listen to the conversation. Then listen and repeat.

A: Is Sam there?

B: I think you have the wrong number.

A: Is this 555-1212 ?

B: No, it isn't.

A: Sorry to bother you.

B: No problem. Bye.

Practice the conversation with a partner.
Use these items.

1	2	3	4	5
Anna / 555-4938	Mr. Wu / 555-3957	Lisa / 555-2468	Ms. Fallon / 555-3000	

2 Practice the Conversation: Answering the Phone

Listen to the conversation. Then listen and repeat.

A: Is Ann there?

B: Who's calling please?

A: This is Pat . I'm her classmate .

B: Just a minute, please. I'll get her.

Practice the conversation with a partner.
Use these items.

1	2	3	4	5
Sue / I play soccer with her.	Dan / I'm her teacher.	Maria / I play cards with her.	Dr. Smith / I'm her dentist.	

3 Practice the Conversation: Taking a Message 🎧

Listen to the conversation. Then listen and repeat

A: Can I speak to your father, please?

B: He's not here now. Can I take a message?

A: Can you ask him to call Mr. Rogers ?
My number is 555-3598 .

B: Call Mr. Rogers at 555-3598 .

A: Right. Thank you.

B: You're welcome. Good-bye.

Practice the conversation with a partner.
Use these items

1 Jeff / 555-2764	2 Dr. Smith / 555-4930	3 Ms. Tanaka / 555-0217	4 Mrs. Garcia / 555-1020	5
Jeff / 555-2764	Dr. Smith / 555-4930	Ms. Tanaka / 555-0217	Mrs. Garcia / 555-1020	

WINDOW ON PRONUNCIATION
Linking Consonant to Vowel 🎧

A Listen to the words. Then listen and repeat.

1. Sam is
2. ask him
3. this is
4. I'm her
5. can I
6. is Ann
7. with Ann
8. just a

B Listen to the sentences. Then listen and repeat.

1. Can I speak to Mike Elliot, please?

2. Can you ask him to call Pat Adams?

3. My number is 555–1234.

4. Wait a minute.

5. His name is Bob Underwood.

Work with a partner. Circle the linking words in the sentences above.

EXAMPLE: 1. (Can I) speak to (Mike Elliot), please?

FAMILY

6

LESSON

The Garcia Family's Expenses

1 Learn New Words 🎧

Look at the pictures below. Listen to the words. Then listen and repeat.

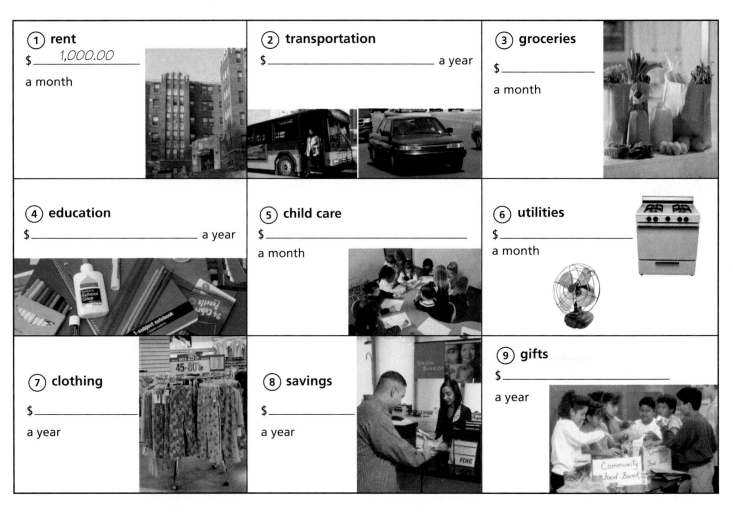

① rent
$ _____1,000.00_____
a month

② transportation
$_____ a year

③ groceries
$_____
a month

④ education
$_____ a year

⑤ child care
$_____
a month

⑥ utilities
$_____
a month

⑦ clothing
$_____
a year

⑧ savings
$_____
a year

⑨ gifts
$_____
a year

2 Give Opinions 🎧

Work with a partner. How much does the Garcia family spend on their expenses? Use these amounts. Write your ideas above.

$75.00	$240.00	$800.00	$1,000.00	$2,000.00
$200.00	$300.00	$900.00	$1,500.00	

Listen to a conversation with Mr. Garcia. Check your guesses.

3 Answer the Questions

Work with a partner. Answer the questions below.

1. How much does the Garcia family spend every year? Write the amounts below.

   rent for a year: _$1,000.00 × 12 = $12,000.00_

   transportation for a year: _____

   groceries for a year: _____

   education for a year: _____

   child care for a year: _____

   utilities for a year: _____

   clothing for a year: _____

   Total: _____

2. Write the Garcia's yearly expenses in order from the most expensive to the least expensive.

   most expensive   _____rent_____
   ($$$$)   _____

                     _____

                     _____

                     _____

                     _____

   least expensive   _____
   ($)

3. What other expenses do you think the Garcias have? Share ideas with your class.

4 Make a Budget

What are your expenses? Complete the chart below.

MY EXPENSES	AMOUNT/MONTH	AMOUNT/YEAR
groceries	$400.00	$4,800.00
	Total:	

What do you know?

1 Listening Review 🎧

Look at the family tree. Listen and choose the best answer. Use the Answer Sheet.

1. A. Bob

   B. Jack

   C. Stephan

2. A. She's Jack's daughter.

   B. She's Jack's wife.

   C. She's Jack's mother.

3. A. She's Tim's mother.

   B. She's Tim's grandmother.

   C. She's Tim's sister.

4. A. Carol

   B. Mei

   C. Ann

Carol Bob
Jack Mei
Ann Tim

Listen and choose the best answer. Use the Answer Sheet.

5. A. No, I don't.

   B. Yes, they do.

   C. Yes, she does.

6. A. It's John.

   B. He's my brother.

   C. He lives in New York.

7. A. Yes, they do.

   B. Yes, there are.

   C. Yes, he does.

8. A. She's my daughter.

   B. She makes the beds.

   C. My children do.

9. A. He lives with me.

   B. They live in New York.

   C. Yes, they are.

10. A. No, she doesn't.

   B. She cooks dinner.

   C. She lives in Florida.

11. A. Yes, I do.

   B. She doesn't.

   C. Yes, please.

12. A. They do.

   B. They often do.

   C. in the morning

ANSWER SHEET

	A	B	C
1	Ⓐ	Ⓑ	Ⓒ
2	Ⓐ	Ⓑ	Ⓒ
3	Ⓐ	Ⓑ	Ⓒ
4	Ⓐ	Ⓑ	Ⓒ
5	Ⓐ	Ⓑ	Ⓒ
6	Ⓐ	Ⓑ	Ⓒ
7	Ⓐ	Ⓑ	Ⓒ
8	Ⓐ	Ⓑ	Ⓒ
9	Ⓐ	Ⓑ	Ⓒ
10	Ⓐ	Ⓑ	Ⓒ
11	Ⓐ	Ⓑ	Ⓒ
12	Ⓐ	Ⓑ	Ⓒ

2 Conversation Check: Pair Work

Student A: Go to page 167.

Student B: Ask your partner questions to complete this chart.

EXAMPLE: **B:** Who's John?

A: He's Bob's father.

Bob's Family

Name	Relationship	Where does he/she live?	What does he/she do for fun?
1. John	Bob's father	California	
2. Cora	Bob's grandmother		plays cards
3. Jodie		California	
4. Lisa	Bob's wife	Florida	plays the guitar
5. Beth	Bob's sister		plays basketball
6. Richard	Bob's brother	Florida	

✔

How many questions did you ask your partner?	How many questions did you answer?
☐ 1 ☐ 2 ☐ 3 ☐ 4 ☐ 5 ☐ 6 ☐ 7	☐ 1 ☐ 2 ☐ 3 ☐ 4 ☐ 5 ☐ 6 ☐ 7

✔ LEARNING LOG

I know these words:

- ☐ aunt
- ☐ brother
- ☐ budget
- ☐ buy the groceries
- ☐ child care
- ☐ children
- ☐ clean the house
- ☐ clothing
- ☐ cook dinner
- ☐ dance
- ☐ daughter

- ☐ do the laundry
- ☐ education
- ☐ expense
- ☐ father
- ☐ fix things
- ☐ gift
- ☐ granddaughter
- ☐ grandfather
- ☐ grandmother
- ☐ grandson
- ☐ groceries

- ☐ husband
- ☐ listen to music
- ☐ make the bed
- ☐ mother
- ☐ parents
- ☐ pay the bills
- ☐ play an instrument
- ☐ play cards
- ☐ play soccer
- ☐ read the newspaper
- ☐ rent

- ☐ savings
- ☐ sister
- ☐ son
- ☐ take out the trash
- ☐ take pictures
- ☐ tell stories
- ☐ transportation
- ☐ uncle
- ☐ utilities
- ☐ wash the dishes
- ☐ wife

I can ask:

- ☐ What's your mother's name?
- ☐ Do you live with your parents?
- ☐ Does he have children?
- ☐ Does your family play cards?
- ☐ Who's calling, please?

I can say:

- ☐ No, I don't.
- ☐ Yes, he does.
- ☐ I usually cook dinner.
- ☐ He washes the dishes.

I can write:

- ☐ about my family
- ☐ a budget

Spotlight: Grammar

SIMPLE PRESENT STATEMENTS

Regular verbs

I
You
We   **live** in California.   He   **lives** in Illinois.
They   **don't live** in New York.   She   **doesn't live** in Maine.

Irregular verbs

I
You
We   **have** two sisters.   He   **has** two sisters.
They   **don't have** two brothers.   She   **doesn't have** two brothers.

1 Complete the sentences. Write *don't* or *doesn't*.

1. My sister lives with my mother. She _____ *doesn't* _____ live with me.

2. We eat a lot of rice. We _____ eat a lot of bread.

3. I have three sons. I _____ have any daughters.

4. I go to work from Monday to Friday. I _____ go to work on Saturday.

5. My daughter goes to school in the morning. She _____ go to school in the afternoon.

6. I get up early in the morning. I _____ get up late.

7. John always has a big breakfast. He _____ have a big dinner.

2 Complete the conversations. Then practice with a partner.

1. A: Do you live with your parents?

   B: No, I _____ *don't* _____. I
      _____ *live* _____ with my brother.

2. A: Do you have a job?

   B: Yes, I _____.
      I _____ a job in a bank.

3. A: Does your father live here?

   B: No, he _____.
      He _____ in China.

4. A: Do you usually cook dinner?

   B: No, I _____. My
      husband usually _____ dinner.

INFORMATION QUESTIONS WITH THE SIMPLE PRESENT

What	**do**	I need for school?	What	**does**	he need for school?
Where	**do**	you live?	Where	**does**	she live?
When	**do**	they usually leave?	When	**does**	it usually leave?
Why	**do**	you live there?	Why	**does**	he live there?
Who	**do**	we know in Miami?	Who	**does**	she live with?
How many sisters	**do**	they have?	How many sisters	**does**	your mother have?

3 Complete the questions. Write *do* or *does*. Then answer the questions.

1. Where _____ *does* _____ your teacher live?

2. When _____ you leave class?

3. How many brothers _____ your mother have?

4. Who _____ you usually eat dinner with?

5. What _____ your family do for fun?

6. How much _____ a pound of chicken cost?

4 Write 4 questions. Then ask a classmate.

1. Where _____

_____

2. When _____

_____

3. Why _____

_____

4. Who _____

_____

Head, Shoulders, Knees, and Toes

THINGS TO DO

1 Learn New Words 🎧

Look at the picture. Listen to the words. Then listen and repeat.

① head   ⑧ toe   ⑮ nose
② neck   ⑨ ankle   ⑯ ear
③ shoulder   ⑩ knee   ⑰ mouth
④ arm   ⑪ stomach   ⑱ chest
⑤ hand   ⑫ throat   ⑲ back
⑥ leg   ⑬ eye   ⑳ wrist
⑦ foot*   ⑭ elbow   ㉑ finger

*Note: The plural of *foot* is *feet*.

2 Write

Add the words above to this chart.

I have one . . .	I have two . . .	I have ten . . .
head	*arms*	

3 Practice the Conversation 🎧

Listen to the conversation. Then listen and repeat.

A: What's the problem?
B: My knee hurts.
A: Is it broken?
B: No, I don't think so.

Practice the conversation with a partner. Use these body parts.

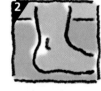
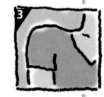

WINDOW ON GRAMMAR
Can for Ability

A Read the questions and answers.

QUESTIONS	ANSWERS
Can you touch your toes?	Yes I **can**. / No, I **can't**.
Can she stand on her head?	Yes, she **can**. / No, she **can't**.

B Answer the questions with *Yes, I can.* or *No, I can't.*

1. Can you touch your toes? _____

2. Can you stand on your head? _____

3. Can you touch your back with your foot? _____

4. Can you stand on one foot for 10 minutes? _____

117

3 LESSON

Put ice on it.

THINGS TO DO

1 Learn New Words 🎧

Look at the pictures. Listen to the words. Then listen and repeat.

1. Drink liquids.
2. Eat soft food.
3. Take cough medicine.
4. Take aspirin.
5. Use ear drops.
6. Rest.
7. Put heat on it.
8. Put ice on it.
9. Bandage it.
10. Keep it dry.

Write the words above the pictures.

2 Interview

Interview a partner. Write your partner's answers.

What do you do for a _____ ?	
stomachache	_eat rice_
headache	
sore throat	
cough	
backache	

Share your partner's answers with the class.

EXAMPLE: My partner eats rice for a stomachache.

3 Practice the Conversation 🎧

Listen to the conversation. Then listen and repeat.

A: What's the problem?

B: I have a sore throat .

A: Are you drinking liquids ?

B: Yes, I am.

Practice the conversation with a partner. Use these problems.

① _____ Drink liquids. _____

⑩ _____

⑨ _____

⑧ _____

③ _____

④ _____

⑤ _____

⑥ _____

⑦ _____

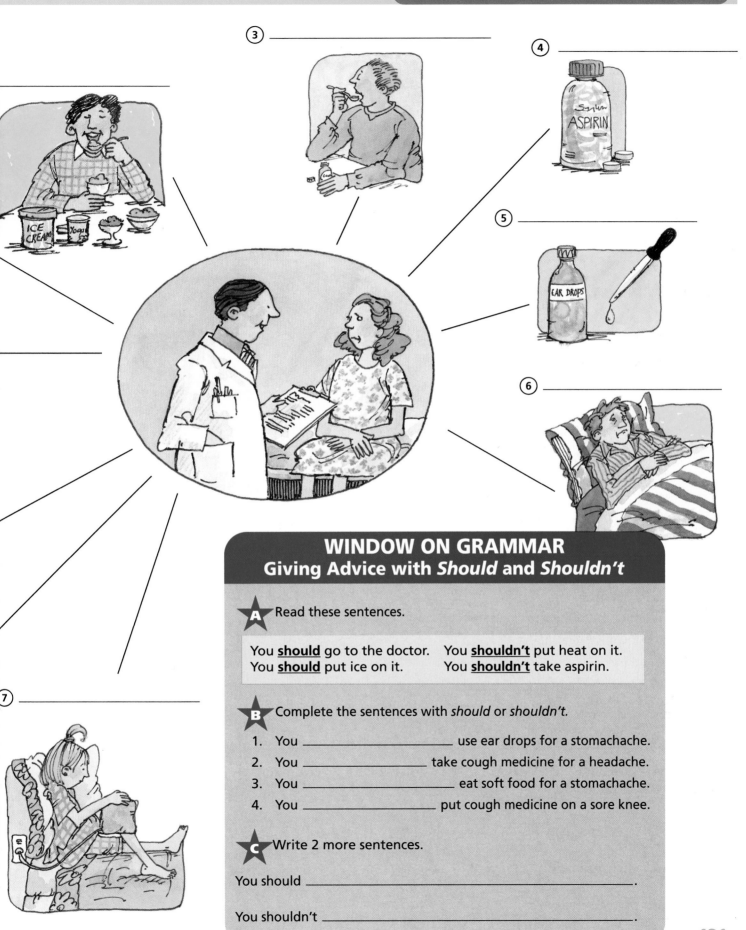

WINDOW ON GRAMMAR
Giving Advice with *Should* and *Shouldn't*

A Read these sentences.

> You **should** go to the doctor.   You **shouldn't** put heat on it.
> You **should** put ice on it.   You **shouldn't** take aspirin.

B Complete the sentences with *should* or *shouldn't*.

1. You _____ use ear drops for a stomachache.
2. You _____ take cough medicine for a headache.
3. You _____ eat soft food for a stomachache.
4. You _____ put cough medicine on a sore knee.

C Write 2 more sentences.

You should _____.

You shouldn't _____.

121

4 LESSON

Safety Warnings

THINGS TO DO

1 Learn New Words

Look at the pictures below. Listen to the words. Then listen and repeat.

① **Flammable!** 	② **Poison!**	③ **Do not take internally.**
④ **Keep out of reach of children.** 	⑤ **Pregnant women should not use this.**	

Write the safety warnings under the pictures.

① _____

② _____

2 Read

Read the warning labels. Check (✓) True or False.

	True	False
1. Children should take aspirin for the flu.	☐	☑
2. Paint remover is flammable.	☐	☐
3. Bleach is a poison.	☐	☐
4. Pregnant women shouldn't use bleach.	☐	☐
5. You should keep ammonia out of reach of children.	☐	☐

3 Write

Make a chart like this. Work with a partner. Write 4 things on each side of the chart.

Things that are poisonous	Things you should keep out of reach of children
gasoline	

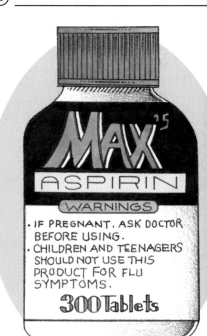

⑤ _____

_____

NET
96 Fl.oz. Samson's (3 QTS.)
2.84 L.
BLEACH
• WARNING •
• AVOID CONTACT WITH EYES
• DO NOT TAKE INTERNALLY
IF SWALLOWED, RINSE MOUTH. DRINK A
GLASS OF WATER CALL PHYSICIAN OR
POISON CONTROL CENTER.

Lemon Scent
AMMONIA
WARNING
KEEP OUT OF
REACH OF
CHILDREN
DO NOT TAKE
INTERNALLY
2.8 Fl.oz. (1 PT. 12 OZ)
828 ML

③ _____

④ _____

_____

WINDOW ON MATH
Gallons, Quarts, Pints, Cups, and Ounces

gallon   *quart*   *pint*   *cup*

1 gallon (gal.)	=	4 quarts (qt.)
1 quart (qt.)	=	2 pints (pt.)
1 pint (pt.)	=	2 cups (c.) = 16 fluid ounces (fl. oz.)

A Complete the sentences.

1. 2 quarts = 4 pints = ___8___ cups = _____ ounces

2. 1 gallon = 4 quarts = _____ pints = _____ cups

3. 2 gallons = _____ quarts = _____ pints = _____ ounces

B Answer the questions.

Which bottle should you buy?
Why?

1 GAL.   3 QTS.   96 OZ.

LESSON 1

Their new house has 3 bedrooms.

THINGS TO DO

1 Learn New Words 🎧

Look at the pictures. Listen to the words. Then listen and repeat.

① sofa   ⑦ sink   ⑬ closet
② bookcase   ⑧ shower   ⑭ refrigerator
③ lamp   ⑨ toilet   ⑮ stove
④ smoke alarm   ⑩ bathtub   ⑯ dresser
⑤ carpet   ⑪ drawer   ⑰ bed
⑥ mirror   ⑫ cabinet

2 Write

Write about the pictures.

1. There are _____*closets*_____ in the kitchen and the bedroom.

2. There is a _____ in the _____ next to the dresser.

3. The refrigerator is in the _____ next to the _____.

4. There are sinks in the _____ and the _____.

5. There are bookcases in the _____ and the _____.

★ ★

TRY THIS Choose a room in your home. List 4 things in it.

> EXAMPLE:
> Room: bedroom
> Things: 3 beds, dresser, lamp, bookcase

Write about the room. Then read your sentences to the class. Your classmates can guess the room.

> EXAMPLE: There is a dresser, a lamp, and a bookcase in this room. There are also 3 beds.

★ ★

Living room

Dining room

Bathroom

Kitchen

Bedroom

WINDOW ON GRAMMAR
Comparing Past and Present

A Read the sentences.

	Past	Present
	Our old house **had** a bathtub.	Our new house **has** a shower.
	Our old house **was** small.	Our new house **is** big.

B Complete the sentences with *has* or *had*.

1. My new house _____ three bedrooms.

2. My old house _____ two bedrooms.

3. She _____ a one-bedroom house last year.

4. This year she _____ a two-bedroom house.

C Complete the sentences with *is* or *was*.

1. My brother _____ in the United States last year.

2. This year he _____ in Mexico.

133

LESSON 2

The Lees' old house had a garage.

THINGS TO DO

1 Learn New Words 🎧

Look at the pictures. Listen to the words. Then listen and repeat.

① pool   ④ carport   ⑦ porch

② patio   ⑤ driveway   ⑧ backyard

③ front yard   ⑥ garage   ⑨ garden

2 Talk About the Pictures

Write 5 sentences about each picture. Share your ideas with a partner.

EXAMPLES: Picture A
Dave and Lucy are playing basketball.

Picture B
The Lees' old house had a garden.

3 Compare

Make a diagram like this. Add 3 things to each part of the diagram. Then share ideas with your class.

The Lees' new house has	Both houses have	The Lees' old house had
a pool	*a driveway*	*a garage*

Which house do you like? Why?

★ ☆ ★ ☆ ★ ☆ ★ ☆ ★ ☆ ★ ☆ ★ ☆ ★ ☆ ★ ☆ ★ ☆ ★ ☆ ★ ☆ ★ ☆ ★ ☆ ★ ☆

TRY THIS   Describe your dream house. Write 4 sentences. Then tell a partner.

EXAMPLE: My dream house has. . . .

It doesn't have. . . .

★ ☆ ★ ☆ ★ ☆ ★ ☆ ★ ☆ ★ ☆ ★ ☆ ★ ☆ ★ ☆ ★ ☆ ★ ☆ ★ ☆ ★ ☆ ★ ☆ ★ ☆

Picture B: The Lees' Old House

Picture A:
The Lees'
New House

3
LESSON

He fell down the stairs.

THINGS TO DO

1 Learn New Words 🎧

Look at the pictures. Listen to the words. Then listen and repeat.

① **fell down the stairs**　　④ **slipped in the shower**
② **fell off a ladder**　　　　⑤ **cut his hand with a knife**
③ **fell off a chair**　　　　⑥ **tripped on the carpet**

Write the words under the pictures.

2 Practice the Conversation

Listen to the conversation. Then listen and repeat.

A: What happened to Joe ?
B: He fell down the stairs.
A: Is he okay now?
B: Yes, I think so.

Work with a partner. Ask about the people in the pictures.

| **1** Mike | **2** Nick | **3** Carol | **4** Donna |

3 Read

Read the bar graph. Answer the questions.

QUESTIONS	ANSWERS
1. How many people got hurt when they fell down the stairs in 2000?	1,050,000
2. How many people got hurt with knives?	
3. How many people got hurt when they fell off chairs?	
4. How many people got hurt when they tripped on a carpet?	

What happened to Joe?

① He _____.

What happened to Sylvia?

② She _____.

What happened to Carol?

③ She _____.

What happened to Mike?

TALK ABOUT IT: Understanding a Bar Graph

What happened to Nick?

(4) He _____ .

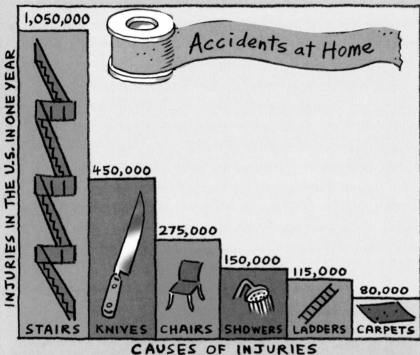

Accidents at Home

INJURIES IN THE U.S. IN ONE YEAR

- 1,050,000 — STAIRS
- 450,000 — KNIVES
- 275,000 — CHAIRS
- 150,000 — SHOWERS
- 115,000 — LADDERS
- 80,000 — CARPETS

CAUSES OF INJURIES

The Amazing Almanac, Blackbirch Press (Woodbridge, CT © 2000)

(5) He _____ .

What happened to Donna?

(6) She _____ .

WINDOW ON GRAMMAR
Simple Past: Regular and Irregular Verbs

A ⭐ Read the sentences.

REGULAR VERBS

Base Form	Past Form	Examples
like	lik**ed**	I lik**ed** my old house.
work	work**ed**	I work**ed** here last year.

IRREGULAR VERBS

Base Form	Past Form	Examples
fall	**fell**	He **fell** down yesterday.
get	**got**	She **got** hurt last week.
cut	**cut**	I **cut** my hand last night.
go	**went**	I **went** home last year.

B ⭐ Complete the sentences with the past form of the verb.

1. They _____ their old house.
   (like)

2. Joan _____ down the stairs yesterday.
   (fall)

3. She _____ in a hospital in 2003.
   (work)

4. I _____ to Mexico last month.
   (go)

5. He _____ a good job last week.
   (get)

137

LESSON 4

Housing Ads

THINGS TO DO

1 Learn New Words 🎧

Look at the pictures. Listen to the words. Then listen and repeat.

① **apartment**　　② **condo**　　③ **mobile home**

2 Write 🎧

Read and listen to the classified ads. Find and write the abbreviations for these words.

WORD	ABBREVIATION(S)
1. apartment	_apt_
2. bathroom	_____
3. bedroom	_____
4. near	_____
5. month	_____
6. garage	_____

3 Read

Read the ads. Answer the questions. Write the letters of the ads.

1. Which places are near schools?　　Ad: _a, g_

2. Which places rent for under $900.00?　Ad: _____

3. Which place costs the most money?　Ad: _____

4. Which places have patios?　　Ad: _____

5. Which place is interesting to you?
   Why?　　　　　　　　　　　Ad: _____

   _____

★ ★

⭐ **TRY THIS** Write a classified ad for your dream house.

FOR SALE
3 bed, 2 bath, . . .

★ ★

---

a
House for Rent
3 bed/2 bath
nr schools
patio and pool
$1350/mo
Call Eileen at
555–4000

b
For Rent
Mobile Home
1 bed, 1 bath
Nr public pool
$795/mo
Call Joe 555–1928

c
House for Sale
3BR, 2BA, big kitchen, 2 fireplaces, patio, gar, $210,000
Call Marlene 555–1200, ext. 15

d
FOR RENT
2 Br, 2 BA apt.
pool & patio
$950
call John
555–4583

e
FOR SALE
2 bed, 1.5 bath condo
nr stores
$175,000
Call Smith Realty 555–6767

REALTY

C6

S H O W C A S E

f Apartment for Rent

1 bed, 1 bath
$825/mo
Call 555-9904

g Condo for Rent

2 bed, 1 bath,
gar, nr schools
$1100/mo
Call Bev 555-4954

h Mobile Home for Rent

2 bed, 1 bth,
patio, no pets
$875/month
call 555-9948

WINDOW ON GRAMMAR
Simple Past Statements: Negative and Affirmative

A Read the sentences.

I **didn't rent** a condo last year. I **rented** a house.
They **didn't buy** a house in 2001. They **bought** a condo.
He **didn't hurt** his hand yesterday. He **hurt** his foot.
She **didn't go** to Miami last week. She **went** to L.A.

B Complete the sentences.

1. They _____*didn't rent*_____ a house last year. They
   <u>rented</u> a condo.

2. Joan _____ down the stairs last week.
   She <u>fell</u> off a ladder.

3. Bob _____ the mobile home. He <u>liked</u>
   the apartment.

4. I _____ my hand. I <u>hurt</u> my foot.

139

LESSON 5

I'm calling about the house.

1 Practice the Conversation: Calling about a House

Listen to the conversation. Then listen and repeat.

A: I'm calling about the house for rent. Is it still available?

B: Yes, it is.

A: Can you tell me, does it have a front yard?

B: Yes, it does.

Practice the conversation with a partner.
Use these items.

1 apartment / a garden	2 condo / a patio	3 mobile home/ a dining room	4 house / a pool	5

2 Practice the Conversation: Asking about Rooms

Listen to the conversation. Then listen and repeat.

A: How many bedrooms does it have?

B: Three.

A: And how many bathrooms?

B: Two.

Practice the conversation with a partner.
Use these items.

1 Two / One and one-half	2 One / One	3 Two small ones / One	4 Four, ... no, five / Three	5 

3 Practice the Conversation: Asking about Rent 🎧

Listen to the conversation. Then listen and repeat.

A: How much is the rent?

B: $1,200.00 a month.

A: Does it include utilities?

B: No, it doesn't.

Practice the conversation with a partner.
Use these items.

 1
$950.00

 2
$825.00

 3
$400.00

 4
$2,200.00

 5

WINDOW ON PRONUNCIATION 🎧
Stress in Compound Nouns

 A Listen to the words. Then listen and repeat.

1. <u>book</u>case	3. bedroom	5. bathroom	7. bathtub	9. mailbox
2. carport	4. fireplace	6. grandson	8. drugstore	10. headache

Underline the part of the word that is stressed. For example: <u>book</u>case.

 B Work with a partner. Ask and answer the questions. Use the words in Activity A.

1. Where can you mail letters?

2. Where can you buy medicine?

3. Where do you sleep?

4. Where do you take a shower?

5. Where can you put books?

6. Who is your daughter's son?

7. If your head hurts, what do you have?

8. Where do you put your car?

9. Where do you take a bath?

10. Where do you make a fire in your home?

Paying Bills

1 Learn New Words 🎧

Look at the bills below. Listen to the words. Then listen and repeat.

① **account number**
② **amount due**
③ **amount enclosed**
④ **new charges**

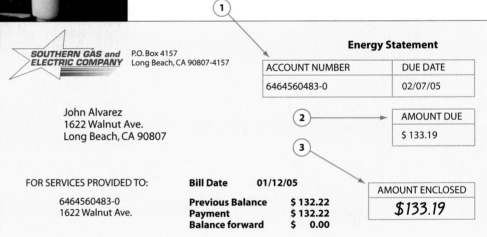

SOUTHERN GAS and ELECTRIC COMPANY
P.O. Box 4157
Long Beach, CA 90807-4157

Energy Statement

ACCOUNT NUMBER	DUE DATE
6464560483-0	02/07/05

John Alvarez
1622 Walnut Ave.
Long Beach, CA 90807

② → | AMOUNT DUE |
| $ 133.19 |

③

FOR SERVICES PROVIDED TO:
6464560483-0
1622 Walnut Ave.

Bill Date   01/12/05
Previous Balance $ 132.22
Payment $ 132.22
Balance forward $ 0.00

| AMOUNT ENCLOSED |
| *$133.19* |

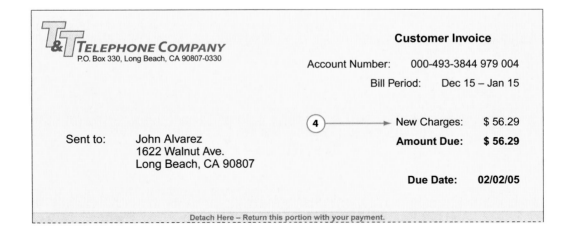

T&T TELEPHONE COMPANY
P.O. Box 330, Long Beach, CA 90807-0330

Customer Invoice

Account Number: 000-493-3844 979 004

Bill Period: Dec 15 – Jan 15

④ →   New Charges: $ 56.29
Amount Due: $ 56.29

Sent to: John Alvarez
1622 Walnut Ave.
Long Beach, CA 90807

Due Date: 02/02/05

Detach Here – Return this portion with your payment.

2 Read

Read the sentences below. Check (✔) True or False.

	True	False
1. John's account number with the gas and electric company is 000-493-3844 979 004.	☐	☐
2. John is paying the gas and electric company $133.19.	☐	☐
3. John's phone bill is for one month.	☐	☐
4. John's account number with the telephone company is 000-493-3844 979 004.	☐	☐
5. The due date for the telephone bill is February 5.	☐	☐

3 Write

Complete the checks. Use the bills from Activity 1.

JOHN ALVAREZ
1622 Walnut Ave.
Long Beach, CA 90807

1129

DATE _____

PAY TO THE ORDER OF _Southern Gas and Electric Company_ $ _____

_____ DOLLARS

FIRST NATIONAL BANK of CALIFORNIA
Los Angeles, California

MEMO _____

⑈012345678⑈: 123ⁱⁱⁱ456 7ⁱⁱ 1129

JOHN ALVAREZ
1622 Walnut Ave.
Long Beach, CA 90807

1130

DATE _____

PAY TO THE ORDER OF _____ $ _____

_____ DOLLARS

FIRST NATIONAL BANK of CALIFORNIA
Los Angeles, California

MEMO _____

⑈012345678⑈: 123ⁱⁱⁱ456 7ⁱⁱ 1130

7 LESSON

What do you know?

1 Listening Review 🎧

Listen to the conversations. Choose the correct picture. Use the Answer Sheet.

1.

   A   B   C

2.

   A   B   C

3.

   A   B   C

4.
 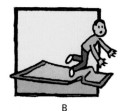 

   A   B   C

ANSWER SHEET

1	Ⓐ	Ⓑ	Ⓒ
2	Ⓐ	Ⓑ	Ⓒ
3	Ⓐ	Ⓑ	Ⓒ
4	Ⓐ	Ⓑ	Ⓒ
5	Ⓐ	Ⓑ	Ⓒ
6	Ⓐ	Ⓑ	Ⓒ
7	Ⓐ	Ⓑ	Ⓒ
8	Ⓐ	Ⓑ	Ⓒ

Listen and choose the best answer. Use the Answer Sheet.

5. A. They're on the table.
   B. It's in the living room.
   C. It's for rent.

6. A. No, it has a shower.
   B. Yes, it has a bathtub.
   C. No, it has a bathtub.

7. A. Yes, they do.
   B. No. We live in a mobile home.
   C. Yes, it is.

8. A. It has a yard.
   B. $500.00
   C. two

144

2 Conversation Check: Pair Work

Student A: Go to page 168.

Student B: Ask your partner questions to complete this chart.

EXAMPLE: **B:** How many rooms are in the White House?

A: There are 132 rooms in the White House.

The U.S. President lives in the White House.

The White House
1600 Pennsylvania Avenue NW
Washington, D.C. 20500

1. Number of rooms:	132	5. Number of elevators:	
2. Number of bathrooms:	35	6. Number of swimming pools:	1
3. Number of doors:		7. Number of movie theaters:	
4. Number of fireplaces:	28	8. Number of windows:	147

✔ | How many questions did you ask your partner? □ 1 □ 2 □ 3 □ 4 | How many questions did you answer? □ 1 □ 2 □ 3 □ 4 |

✔ LEARNING LOG

I know these words:

□ accident
□ account number
□ amount due
□ amount enclosed
□ apartment
□ backyard
□ bathroom
□ bathtub
□ bed
□ bedroom
□ bookcase

□ cabinet
□ carpet
□ carport
□ closet
□ condo
□ cut (his hand) with a knife
□ dining room
□ drawer
□ dresser
□ driveway

□ fall
□ fell
□ front yard
□ garage
□ garden
□ kitchen
□ ladder
□ lamp
□ living room
□ mirror
□ mobile home

□ new charges
□ patio
□ pool
□ porch
□ refrigerator
□ sale
□ shower
□ sink
□ slip
□ slipped
□ smoke alarm

□ sofa
□ stairs
□ stove
□ toilet
□ trip
□ tripped

I can ask:

□ What happened to Joe?
□ Does it have a yard?
□ How much is the rent?

I can say:

□ There is a closet in the room.
□ Our new house has a bathtub.
□ Our old house had a shower.
□ We liked our old house.
□ We didn't buy a house last year.

I can write:

□ checks to pay bills

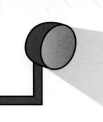

Spotlight: Grammar

SIMPLE PAST STATEMENTS		
REGULAR VERBS	**IRREGULAR VERBS**	**VERB BE**
I He She It You We They ⟩ **worked** yesterday. **didn't work** last week.	I He She It You We They ⟩ **went** by plane. **didn't go** by train.	I He She It ⟩ **was** in class yesterday. **wasn't** at home. You We They ⟩ **were** in class yesterday. **weren't** at home.

1 Write about yesterday.

1. She has shrimp for dinner every day.
   _____*She had shrimp for dinner*_____ yesterday.

2. He buys a pint of milk every day.
   _____ yesterday.

3. I make the beds every day.
   _____ yesterday.

4. My friends are here every day.
   _____ yesterday.

5. The weather is terrible every day.
   _____ yesterday.

6. He eats six servings of vegetables every day.
   _____ yesterday.

7. I get up before 7:00 every day.
   _____ yesterday.

8. I run to the bus stop every day.
   _____ yesterday.

IRREGULAR VERBS	
buy	bought
come	came
cost	cost
drink	drank
get up	got up
go	went
have	had
hurt	hurt
is / are	was / were
eat	ate
leave	left
make	made
meet	met
run	ran
see	saw
sleep	slept
spend	spent

2 Write 5 sentences about what you did yesterday. Use the words in the box.

got up	ate	went	saw
didn't go	was	had	slept

INFORMATION QUESTIONS WITH THE SIMPLE PAST		
What	**did**	you eat for breakfast?
Where	**did**	we meet them?
When	**did**	they leave for work?
Why	**did**	she leave yesterday?
Who	**did**	he meet at the party?
How much bread	**did**	your children eat yesterday?
How many apples	**did**	they eat yesterday?

3 Match the questions and answers. Then practice with a partner.

1. _e_ Where did you go yesterday?
2. ___ What did you eat this morning?
3. ___ How many glasses of water did you drink yesterday?
4. ___ How many hours did you sleep last night?
5. ___ How much money did you spend yesterday?
6. ___ Who did you dance with last?
7. ___ Who did you call on the telephone yesterday?
8. ___ When did you leave your house this morning?

a. I called my daughter.
b. I left at 8:00.
c. I slept five hours.
d. I ate a banana.
e. I went to work.
f. I drank eight glasses of water.
g. I spent $10.00.
h. I danced with my wife.

4 Complete the conversations. Then practice with a partner.

1. A: Where _____did_____ you go yesterday?
   B: I _____ to the movies.

2. A: What movie _____ you see?
   B: I _____ a new Chinese movie.

3. A: Did you like it?
   B: Yes, I did. I _____ it a lot.

4. A: What _____ you eat yesterday?
   B: I _____ a lot of fruits and vegetables.

5. A: _____ you eat any meat?
   B: No, I _____.

6. A: Did you buy anything yesterday?
   B: Yes, I did. I _____ a new sweater.

7. A: How much _____ it cost?
   B: It _____ $25.00.

UNIT 10: Work

1 LESSON

Can you use a computer?

THINGS TO DO

1 Learn New Words 🎧

Look at the pictures. Listen to the words. Then listen and repeat.

1. chef
2. office manager
3. plumber
4. stylist
5. child care worker
6. mechanic
7. mover
8. construction worker
9. truck driver
10. landscaper

Write the words above the pictures.

2 Write

Write 5 sentences about your friends and family.

EXAMPLES: My husband can lift heavy things.
My friend Jose can drive a truck.

Read your sentences to the class.

3 Find Someone Who

Talk to your classmates. Find someone who can do each thing. Write the person's name.

A: Can you drive a car ?
B: Yes, I can. / No, I can't.

FIND SOMEONE WHO CAN:	NAME
drive a car	_____
cook rice	_____
lift 50 pounds	_____
use a computer	_____
repair toilets	_____
build a table	_____

Indoor Jobs

1 A _____
cooks food.

2 An _____
_____
uses a computer.

3 A _____
repairs sinks and toilets.

4 A _____
cuts hair.

Outdoor Jobs

⑤ A _____

_____

takes care of children.

⑧ A _____

builds buildings.

Indoor/ Outdoor Jobs

⑥ A _____

fixes cars.

⑨ A _____

drives a truck.

⑦ A _____

lifts heavy things.

⑩ A _____

takes care of plants.

WINDOW ON GRAMMAR
Yes/No Questions + Simple Past

A Read the questions and answers.

QUESTIONS	ANSWERS
Did you work last week?	**Yes, I did**.
Did you drive a car last week?	**No, I didn't**.

B Ask a partner these questions.

1. Did you cook dinner last week?
2. Did you use a computer last month?
3. Did you build furniture last year?
4. Did you drive a truck yesterday?

C Write your own question. Then ask a partner.

Did you

_____?

LESSON 2

Do you have experience?

THINGS TO DO

1 Read

Read the job ads. Take notes in the chart below.

JOB	PART-TIME OR FULL-TIME?	BENEFITS?
Office manager	*full-time*	yes
Construction worker		
Chef		
Child care worker		
Landscaper		
Pharmacist's assistant		

2 Write

Which job do you like? Why? Write 2 sentences. Then tell a partner.

> EXAMPLE: I like the chef job. I like to cook.

3 Practice the Conversation 🎧

Listen to the conversation. Then listen and repeat.

A: I'm calling about the ad for an office manager .

B: Do you have experience?

A: Yes, I do. I have 2 years of experience.

B: Good! Can you come in for an interview tomorrow at 3:00 ?

A: Yes. I'll be there.

Practice the conversation with a partner. Use these items.

1 a landscaper	**2** a child care worker	**3** a stylist	**4** a truck driver
8:00 A.M.	noon	7:30 P.M.	9:00 in the morning

★ ★

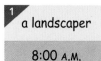 **TRY THIS** Write a help wanted ad for your dream job. Read the ad to your classmates.

★ ★

1

Competitive Wages & Benefits Plenty of Work

CONSTRUCTION WORKERS NEEDED
Call 860–555–3209 and leave message. Full-time work.

4

Full-Time
Help Wanted
Reliable
LANDSCAPERS
Needed.
• Excellent Pay
• Good Benefits
Apply in Person
Spring Look Landscaping
66 River Road
Santa Anita

3

SPS, Inc.
Has an immediate opening for a full-time Office Manager. Benefits include medical insurance and paid vacation. If interested call for an interview.
(503)555–9438

2

Legends Grill
Immediate Opening for Chef
Excellent benefits
Call John for an Interview
4 Corey Drive
212–555–6948

5

Child Care Worker Part-Time
Flexible hours.
Sorry, no benefits.
Call Judy Eno
818–555–9483

6

Allen's Drugstore
Pharmacist's assistant needed. 40 hours a week. Good benefits. Call 430–555–3482 for an interview.

WINDOW ON MATH
Word Problems

 A Work with a partner. Answer these word problems.

1. Sam worked 40 hours a week as a mechanic last month. He earned $20.00 an hour. How much did he earn last month?

2. Taka earns $12.00 an hour as a child care worker. She works Monday, Wednesday, and Friday from 7 A.M. to 4 P.M. How much does she earn a week?

3. Robert is a chef's assistant. He works part-time in two restaurants. He works from 7 A.M. to 1 P.M. Monday through Friday and earns $10.00 an hour. He works from 4 P.M. to 11 P.M. on Saturday and Sunday and earns $15.00 an hour. How much does he earn a week?

3 LESSON

Tell me about yourself.

THINGS TO DO

1 Talk About the Picture

Write 5 things about the picture.

EXAMPLES: People are talking.
The man in the yellow shorts has a dog.

Share your ideas with the class.

2 Listen and Take Notes 🎧

Listen to Rosa's job interview. Write the missing information.

Rosa Perez		
Employer	Job Title	Dates
Lane's	_____	2000 – Present
Lane's	_____	1998 – 2000
The Elephant's Trunk	Salesclerk	_____ – _____

3 Give Opinions

What should you do at a job interview? What shouldn't you do? Make a chart like the one below. Use these ideas. Then add 5 of your own.

be late   dress neatly   chew gum

listen carefully   ask questions   shake hands

AT A JOB INTERVIEW:	
You should . . .	You shouldn't . . .
dress neatly	*be late*

ANNUAL JOB FA

LESSON 4

The Amazing Story of Mr. Kazi

THINGS TO DO

1 Talk About the Pictures

Write 1 sentence about each picture.

> EXAMPLE: The men are cleaning the car in picture 1.

Share your ideas with the class.

2 Read

Read the story. Put the events in order from first (1) to last (6).

_____ He sold 1 restaurant and bought 3 more.

_____ He worked as a chef's assistant.

_____ He managed a fast-food restaurant.

_____ He owns 168 restaurants.

__1__ Mr. Kazi worked at a car rental company.

_____ He bought a fast-food restaurant.

3 Check True or False

Read the sentences below. Check (✔) True or False.

	True	False
1. Mr. Kazi owned a car rental company.	❏	❏
2. He worked full-time as a chef's assistant.	❏	❏
3. Mr. Kazi was a hard worker.	❏	❏
4. Mr. Kazi borrowed money to buy a restaurant.	❏	❏
5. He was born in the U.S.	❏	❏
6. Today he owns many restaurants.	❏	❏

★ ★

TRY THIS Write your story. Write about 5 events in your life. Write the events in order from first to last.

★ ★

1.
Mr. Kazi came to the United States when he was 23 years old. His first job was for a car rental company.

4.
A few years later Mr. Kazi borrowed money from a bank. He bought a fast-food restaurant in very bad condition. He repaired the building and improved the food. He worked seven days a week. Soon the restaurant was making money.

2.
On weekends, Mr. Kazi worked as a chef's assistant at a fast-food restaurant. He cleaned the kitchen and helped the chef.

3.
Mr. Kazi worked very hard in the restaurant. Soon the owners of the restaurant promoted him to restaurant manager. He managed the restaurant for the next three years.

5.
A year later Mr. Kazi sold his restaurant. With the money he earned, he bought three more restaurants.

6.
Today Mr. Kazi is the owner of 168 restaurants. He is going to buy more restaurants in the future.

WINDOW ON GRAMMAR
Future with *Be going to*

 Read the sentences.

| I | **am going to** look for a new job. |

| He
She
It | **is going to** be in Mexico next year. |

| We
They | **are going to** open a restaurant next month. |

B Complete the sentences.

1. Mr. Kazi ___*is going to buy*___ more restaurants next year.
   (buy)

2. I _____ to Mexico next year.
   (go)

3. They _____ medicine next year.
   (study)

4. She _____ the restaurant next week.
   (manage)

5. We _____ after school next year.
   (work)

LESSON 5

Why did you leave your last job?

1 Practice the Conversation: Talking about Work Experience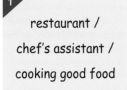

Listen to the conversation. Then listen and repeat.

A: Tell me about your last job.

B: Well, I worked at a department store .
I was a salesclerk .

A: Did you like the job?

B: Yes. I liked helping people .
And there was always something to do.

Practice the conversation with a partner.
Use these items.

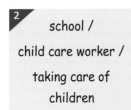

1	2	3	4
restaurant / chef's assistant / cooking good food	school / child care worker / taking care of children	salon / stylist / cutting hair	

2 Practice the Conversation: Talking about Changing Jobs

Listen to the conversation. Then listen and repeat.

A: Why did you leave your last job?

B: I went back to school.

A: I see. And why do you want to work here?

B: I think it's a very good company .

Practice the conversation with a partner.
Use these items.

1	2	3	4
The restaurant closed. / restaurant	My family moved here. / school	I didn't have benefits. / salon	

3 Practice the Conversation: Answering Job Interview Questions 🎧

Listen to the conversation. Then listen and repeat.

A: Why should I hire you?

B: I'm good with people.

A: That's good. We like our employees to be good with people .

B: I'm glad to hear that.

Practice the conversation with a partner.

Use these items.

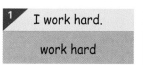 **1** I work hard.

work hard

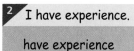 **2** I have experience.

have experience

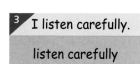 **3** I listen carefully.

listen carefully

4

WINDOW ON PRONUNCIATION 🎧
Stressing Important Words in Sentences

 A Listen to the sentences. Then listen and repeat.

1. Tell me about your last <u>job</u>.

2. I worked at a department store.

3. Why did you leave your last job?

4. Why should I hire you?

Underline the stressed words.

 B Listen to the questions. Underline the stressed words.

1. A: What did you do in your last job?

   B: _____

2. A: Did you like the job?

   B: _____

3. A: Why should I hire you?

   B: _____

4. A: Why do you want to work here?

   B: _____

Work with a partner. Ask and answer the questions.

157

Job Applications

1 Read

Read about Francis Yasine. Then complete the job application below for Francis.

My name is Francis Martin Yasine, and I live at 2435 Melford Avenue in Sacramento, California. In my country, I worked as a mechanic. I liked my job a lot. My friends say I'm a good mechanic. Now I don't have a job. I really want a full-time job.

Job Application
Personal Information

First Name: _____

Middle Initial: _____

Last Name: _____

Birth Date: __6__ / __23__ / __70__

Present Address: _____

City: _____

State: _____

Zip Code: __95652_____

Phone Number: __(916) 555-4938_____

* Are you currently employed?   ☐ Yes ☐ No

* Do you have a valid driver's license?   ☑ Yes ☐ No

* Do you have access to an automobile? ☑ Yes ☐ No

* Number of hours/week desired: _____

* Days and A.M./P.M. hours available:

	Mon.	Tues.	Wed.	Thurs.	Fri.	Sat.	Sun.
A.M.	☑	☑	☑	☑	☑	☑	☐
P.M.	☑	☑	☑	☑	☑	☐	☐

2 Write

Complete this job application with information about yourself.

Job Application
Personal Information

First Name: _____

Middle Initial: _____

Last Name: _____

Birth Date: _____ /_____ /_____

Present Address: _____

City: _____

State: _____

Zip Code: _____

Phone Number: _____

* Are you currently employed?   □ Yes   □ No

* Do you have a valid driver's license?   □ Yes   □ No

* Do you have access to an automobile?   □ Yes   □ No

* Number of hours/week desired: _____

* Days and A.M./P.M. hours available:

	Mon.	Tues.	Wed.	Thurs.	Fri.	Sat.	Sun.
A.M.	□	□	□	□	□	□	□
P.M.	□	□	□	□	□	□	□

3 Interview

Work with a partner. Ask your partner 5 questions about his or her job application.

EXAMPLE: A: Do you have a valid driver's license?
          B: Yes, I do. / No, I don't.

LESSON 7

What do you know?

1 Listening Review 🎧

Listen and choose the correct answer. Use the Answer Sheet.

1. A. They fix cars.
   B. They cut hair.
   C. They take care of children.

2. A. Yes, he can.
   B. No, they can't.
   C. No, he's not.

3. A. Yes, she does.
   B. Yes, she can.
   C. Yes, she did.

4. A. Yes, it is.
   B. Yes, they did.
   C. Yes, she is.

5. A. I worked at a restaurant.
   B. My family moved.
   C. I liked it very much.

6. A. I work very hard.
   B. You shouldn't be late.
   C. Yes, you should.

7. A. $20.00
   B. $200.00
   C. $2,000.00

8. A. $400.00
   B. $800.00
   C. $1,000.00

ANSWER SHEET			
1	A	B	C
2	A	B	C
3	A	B	C
4	A	B	C
5	A	B	C
6	A	B	C
7	A	B	C
8	A	B	C

2 Dictation 🎧

Listen and write the questions you hear.

1. _____

2. _____

3. _____

Answer the questions you wrote above.

1. _____

2. _____

3. _____

3 Conversation Check: Pair Work

Student A: Go to page 168.

Student B: Ask your partner questions about Jane Roe. Answer your partner's questions about Bob Wu.

EXAMPLE:
  B: When did Jane work at Lane's Department Store?

  A: From March 1998 to May 2000.

Jane Roe
1234 Altadena Drive
Altadena, California 91001
626-555-3954   jroe@dayna.net

Work Background

5/2000 to present	*Store Manager*	**Gould's Drugstore**
(3/1998) to 5/2000	*Assistant Manager*	**Lane's Department Store**
7/1995 to 12/1997		**Regina's Boutique**
		Westville Public Library

Bob Wu
5395 Manchester Road
Andover, Illinois 61233
309-555-4503   bbwu@access.net

Work Background

7/2002 to present	*Construction Worker*	**ABC Industries**
9/1995 to 6/2002	*Truck Driver*	**HFC Inc.**
3/1993 to 3/1995	*Landscaper*	**Greenthumbs**
11/1991 to 1/1993	*Cashier*	**Sam's Supermarket**

✔

How many questions did you ask your partner?	How many questions did you answer?
□ 1 □ 2 □ 3 □ 4	□ 1 □ 2 □ 3 □ 4

✔ LEARNING LOG

I know these words:

□ ask questions	□ cook	□ make	□ shake hands
□ be late	□ dress neatly	□ mechanic	□ stylist
□ benefits	□ drive	□ mover	□ take care of
□ build	□ heavy	□ office manager	□ truck driver
□ chef	□ indoor	□ outdoor	
□ chew gum	□ landscaper	□ plumber	
□ child care worker	□ lift	□ reliable	
□ construction worker	□ listen carefully	□ repair	

I can ask:
- □ Can you use a computer?
- □ Did you work last week?
- □ Do you have experience?
- □ Did you like the job?
- □ Why did you leave your last job?

I can say:
- □ Yes, I did.
- □ No, I didn't.
- □ You shouldn't be late.
- □ I'm going to look for a new job.

I can write:
- □ a job application

Conversation Check: Pair Work

Student A: Ask your partner questions to complete the price tags.

EXAMPLE: **A:** What size is the red sweater?
B: It's a large.
A: How much is it?

a. Size: *LARGE*
Price:

b. Size: EXTRA LARGE
Price: $50.00

c. Size:
Price:

d. Size: MEDIUM
Price: $48.00

How many questions did you ask your partner?	How many questions did you answer?
☐ 1 ☐ 2 ☐ 3 ☐ 4	☐ 1 ☐ 2 ☐ 3 ☐ 4

Conversation Check: Pair Work

Student A: Ask your partner questions to complete this chart.

EXAMPLE: **A:** How much is a carton of orange juice?
B: $2.00

	FOOD	PRICE (*How much?*)	SIZE/AMOUNT (*What size?*)
1	WHOLE TOMATOES	$2.50	28 ounces
2	PURE HONEY	$3.00	8 ounces
3	ORANGE JUICE	*$2.00*	
4	OIL		

How many questions did you ask your partner?	How many questions did you answer?
☐ 1 ☐ 2 ☐ 3 ☐ 4	☐ 1 ☐ 2 ☐ 3 ☐ 4

Conversation Check: Pair Work

Student A: Ask your partner questions to complete this chart.

EXAMPLE: **A:** Where does John live?
B: He lives in California.

Bob's Family

Name	Relationship	Where does he/she live?	What does he/she do for fun?
1. John	Bob's father	*California*	takes pictures
2. Cora		Texas	
3. Jodie	Bob's sister		dances
4. Lisa	Bob's wife	Florida	
5. Beth		Texas	
6. Richard	Bob's brother	Florida	plays soccer

✔

How many questions did you ask your partner?	How many questions did you answer?
□ 1 □ 2 □ 3 □ 4 □ 5 □ 6 □ 7	□ 1 □ 2 □ 3 □ 4 □ 5 □ 6 □ 7

Conversation Check: Pair Work

Student A: Ask your partner questions to complete this chart.

EXAMPLE: **A:** What's the matter with Mei?
B: She has a stomachache.
A: What's she doing for it?

Name	What's the matter with him/her?	What's he/she doing for it?
1. Tom		
2. Mei	She has a stomachache.	
3. Lisa		
4. Bob		

How many questions did you ask your partner?
□ 1 □ 2 □ 3 □ 4
How many questions did you answer?
□ 1 □ 2 □ 3 □ 4

Conversation Check: Pair Work

Student A: Ask your partner questions to complete this chart.

EXAMPLE: **A:** How many bathrooms are in the White House?
B: There are 35 bathrooms in the White House.

The U.S. President lives in the White House.

The White House
1600 Pennsylvania Avenue NW
Washington, D.C. 20500

1. Number of rooms:	132	5. Number of elevators:	3
2. Number of bathrooms:	35	6. Number of swimming pools:	
3. Number of doors:	412	7. Number of movie theaters:	1
4. Number of fireplaces:		8. Number of windows:	

How many questions did you ask your partner?	How many questions did you answer?
☐ 1 ☐ 2 ☐ 3 ☐ 4	☐ 1 ☐ 2 ☐ 3 ☐ 4

Conversation Check: Pair Work

Jane Roe
1234 Altadena Drive
Altadena, California 91001
626–555–3954   jroe@dayna.net

Student A: Answer your partner's questions about Jane Roe. Ask your partner questions about Bob Wu.

EXAMPLE: **A:** When did Bob work at HFC Inc.?
B: From September 1995 to June 2002.

Work Background

5/2000 to present	*Store Manager*	**Gould's Drugstore**
3/1998 to 5/2000	*Assistant Manager*	**Lane's Department Store**
7/1995 to 12/1997	*Assistant*	**Regina's Boutique**
9/1993 to 5/1995	*Librarian's Assistant*	**Westville Public Library**

Bob Wu
5395 Manchester Road
Andover, Illinois 61233
309–555–4503   bbwu@access.net

Work Background

7/2002 to present	Construction Worker	**ABC Industries**
9/1995 to 6/2002		**HFC Inc.**
3/1993 to 3/1995		**Greenthumbs**
	Cashier	**Sam's Supermarket**

How many questions did you ask your partner?
☐ 1 ☐ 2 ☐ 3 ☐ 4

How many questions did you answer?
☐ 1 ☐ 2 ☐ 3 ☐ 4

A Present Tense of *Be*

Affirmative Statements

I	am	a student.	We	are	students.
You	are	a student.	You	are	students.
He	is	a student.	They	are	students.
She	is	a student.			
It	is	a book.			

Negative Statements

I	am not	a teacher.	We	are not	teachers.
You	are not	a teacher.	You	are not	teachers.
He	is not	a teacher.	They	are not	teachers.
She	is not	a teacher.			
It	is not	a map.			

Contractions

I am	→	I'm	I am not	→	I'm not
You are	→	You're	You are not	→	You aren't/You're not
He is	→	He's	He is not	→	He isn't/He's not
She is	→	She's	She is not	→	She isn't/She's not
It is	→	It's	It is not	→	It isn't/It's not
We are	→	We're	We are not	→	We aren't/We're not
You are	→	You're	You are not	→	You aren't/You're not
They are	→	They're	They are not	→	They aren't/They're not

Yes/No Questions and Short Answers

Am	I			I	am.		I	'm not.
Are	you			you	are.		you	aren't.
Is	he			he	is.		he	isn't.
Is	she	late?	Yes,	she	is.	No,	she	isn't.
Is	it			it	is.		it	isn't.
Are	we			we	are.		we	aren't.
Are	you			you	are.		you	aren't.
Are	they			they	are.		they	aren't.

Information Questions

Where	am are is is is are are	I? you? he? she? it? we? they?	Who are you? Who is she?	Why are you here? Why is she here?
			What is your name? What is her name?	How are you? How is she?
			When is the party? When are the holidays?	How old are you? How old is she?

B Possessives

Possessive Nouns

To form the possessive of any singular noun, add an apostrophe and *-s*.
Examples: John's book   Amy's map   the teacher's desk

To form the possessive of a plural noun that ends in *-s*, just add an apostrophe.
Examples: the girls' desks   the boys' room

To form the possessive of a plural noun that does not end in *-s*, add an apostrophe and *-s*.
Examples: the children's teacher   the women's team   the men's room

Possessive Adjectives

Here is	my your his her its	paper.		Here is	our your their	book.

C *There is/There are*

Affirmative Statements

There is	one store a bank a park	on State St.		There are	two restaurants several stores lots of people	on Main St.

Negative Statements				
There isn't	a clock in the room. one book here. any paper in my notebook.		There aren't	any books in the room. any cars on the street. any pens by the phone.

Yes/No Questions and Short Answers			
Is there	a clock a window a closet	in your room?	Yes, there is. No, there isn't.
Are there	any books pens notebooks	on the table?	Yes, there are. No, there aren't.

D Simple Present Tense

Affirmative Statements					
I You He She It	like like likes likes likes	music.	We You They	like like like	music.

Negative Statements					
I You He She It	don't like don't like doesn't like doesn't like doesn't like	tea.	We You They	don't like don't like don't like	tea.

Yes/No Questions and Short Answers								
Do	I			I	do.		I	don't.
Do	you			you	do.		you	don't.
Does	he			he	does.		he	doesn't.
Does	she	like milk?	Yes,	she	does.	No,	she	doesn't.
Does	it			it	does.		it	doesn't.
Do	we			we	do.		we	don't.
Do	you			you	do.		you	don't.
Do	they			they	do.		they	don't.

Information Questions

Where	do do does does does do do	I you he she it we they	live?	Who do you live with? Who does she live with?	Why do you smoke? Why does she smoke?
				What do you like? What does she like?	How do you do this? How does she do this?
				When do you get up? When does she get up?	How often do you eat? How often does he eat?

E Present Continuous Tense

Affirmative Statements

I	am working.	We	are working.
You	are working.	You	are working.
He	is working.	They	are working.
She	is working.		
It	is working.		

Negative Statements

I	am not working.	We	aren't working.
You	aren't working.	You	aren't working.
He	isn't working.	They	aren't working.
She	isn't working.		
It	isn't working.		

Yes/No Questions and Short Answers

Am	I			I	am.		I	am not.
Are	you			you	are.		you	aren't.
Is	he			he	is.		he	isn't.
Is	she	working?	Yes,	she	is.	No,	she	isn't.
Is	it			it	is.		it	isn't.
Are	we			we	are.		we	aren't.
Are	you			you	are.		you	aren't.
Are	they			they	are.		they	aren't.

Information Questions

What	am are is is is are are	I you he she it we they	doing?	Who are you talking to? Who is she talking to?	Why are you leaving? Why is she leaving?
				Where are you working? Where is she working?	How are you feeling? How is she feeling?

F Simple Past Tense

Affirmative Statements

I You He She It	worked	yesterday.	We You They	worked	yesterday.

Negative Statements

I You He She It	didn't work	yesterday.	We You They	didn't work	yesterday.

Yes/No Questions and Short Answers

Did	I you he she it we you they	work yesterday?	Yes,	I you he she it we you they	did.	No,	I you he she it we you they	didn't.

Information Questions

Where	did	I you he she it we they	work?	Who did you work with? Who did she talk to?	Why did you go? Why did she leave?
				Who worked yesterday? Who called?	How did you get here? How did she feel?
				When did you arrive? When did she call?	What did you do? What did she say?

Past Tense of Irregular Verbs

buy	bought		eat	ate
come	came		leave	left
cost	cost		make	made
do	did		meet	met
drink	drank		pay	paid
get up	got up		run	ran
go	went		see	saw
have	had		sleep	slept
hurt	hurt		spend	spent
is/are	was/were			

G Nouns

Plural Nouns

To form the plural of:		Examples
most nouns	add -s	book—books student—students
most nouns that end in s, sh, ch, x, or z	add -es	dish—dishes couch—couches
most nouns that end in ay, ey, oy, or uy	add -s	boy—boys day—days
most nouns that end in -f or -fe	change -f to -v and add -es or -s	wife—wives loaf—loaves
most nouns that end in a consonant and -y	change the -y to -i and add -es	story—stories candy—candies
most nouns that end in -o	add -s	radio—radios
some nouns that end in consonant and -o	add -es	potato—potatoes

Note: This audio script offers support for many of the activities in the Student Book. When the words on the Student Book page are identical to those on the audio program, the script is not provided here.

UNIT ONE

Lesson 2. (page 6)
1. Learn New Words
Look at the picture. Listen to the words.
Then listen and repeat.

1. teacher	Where's the teacher?
2. wall	What's on the wall?
3. clock	Where's the clock?
4. door	Where's the door?
5. board	Where's the board?
6. table	Where's the table?
7. calendar	Where's the calendar?
8. map	Where's the map?
9. notebook	Where's the notebook?
10. pen	Where's the pen?
11. pencil	Where's the pencil?
12. piece of paper	Where's the piece of paper?
13. book	Where's the book?
14. floor	What's on the floor?
15. chair	Where's the chair?
16. computer	Where's the computer?
17. desk	Where's the desk?
18. student	Where's the student?
19. window	Where's the window?

Lesson 4. (page 10)
1. Learn New Words
[...]at the picture. Listen to the information.

[...] name is Paul. His middle name is Richard. His
[...]e is Bridges. His address is 8517 Alvarado Street
[...]ngeles, California. The zip code is 91012. Paul's
[...]one number is area code 310-555-5678. His birth-
[...] Sacramento, California in the United States. His
[...] is male. His marital status is married. He's a
[...]r. That's his occupation.

[...]and repeat.

[...]ddle name	10. gender
[...]dress	11. male
[...]eet	12. female
[...]y	13. marital status
[...]te	14. single
[...] code	15. married
[...]lephone number	16. divorced
[...]ea code	17. occupation
[...]rthplace	

[...]n 5. (page 12)
[...]actice the Conversation: Greeting Someone
[...]n to the conversation. Then listen and repeat.
[...]ello. I'm Mr. Campos.
[...]lice to meet you, Mr. Campos. I'm Ms. Jones.
[...]lice to meet you.

[...]n to the new words and expressions. Then repeat.

How do you do?	Hello.
Ms.	Mrs.

Lesson 5. (page 12)
2. Practice the Conversation: Introducing Someone
Listen to the conversation. Then listen and repeat.

A: Hi, Jon. How are you?
B: Fine, thanks. And you?
A: I'm fine. Jon, this is my friend Gina.
B: Hi, Gina. Nice to meet you.

Listen to the new words and expressions. Then repeat.
Good   Not bad   OK   Great
I want to introduce you to Gina.
I want you to meet Gina.
This is Gina.

Lesson 5. (page 13)
3. Practice the Conversation: Saying Good-bye
Listen to the conversation. Then listen and repeat.

A: Good-bye, Jon.
B: Bye, David.
A: You too.

Listen to the new expressions. Then repeat.
Have a nice day.
See you later.
Nice to see you.
Have a great day.
Have a good day.

Lesson 5. (page 13)
Window on Pronunciation
Long Vowel Sounds: *I* and *E*
C. Listen and circle the word you hear.

1. my	my		4. write	write
2. he	he		5. bye	bye
3. E	E		6. we	we

Lesson 6. (page 14)
1. Learn New Words
Look at the pictures below. Listen to the words.
Then listen and repeat.

1. dentist	Joan Baxter is a dentist.
2. bus driver	Larry Fisher is a bus driver.
3. pharmacist	Ken Park is a pharmacist.
4. doctor	Emma Lambert is a doctor.
5. salesclerk	Paul Ming is a salesclerk.
6. machinist	David Campos is a machinist.
7. police officer	Gina Mata is a police officer.
8. nurse	Leo Brunov is a nurse.
9. cashier	Amy Craft is a cashier.

Lesson 5. (page 44)
1. Practice the Conversation: Asking about Business Hours
Listen to the conversation. Then listen and repeat.

A: Hello. Anderson's Drugstore. Can I help you?
B: Yes. What are your hours on Thursday?
A: We're open from eight to six.
B: Thank you.

Lesson 5. (page 44)
2. Practice the Conversation: Calling Directory Assistance
Listen to the conversation. Then listen and repeat.

A: Welcome to Horizon. What city and state?
B: Miami, Florida.
A: What listing?
B: Rafael Hernandez.
A: The number is area code 305-555-5938.

Listen to the new places. Then repeat.

New York, New York   Houston, Texas
Santa Ana, California   Miami, Florida

Lesson 5. (page 45)
3. Listen and Write: Listening to a Recorded Message
Listen and write the missing numbers.
Then listen and check.

Thank you for calling the Coral Beach Public Library. For hours, press 1.
The library is open Monday through Thursday from eleven to nine. On Friday and Saturday, the library is open from nine to five. Good-bye.

Lesson 5. (page 45)
Window on Pronunciation
***Thirteen* or *Thirty*? Syllable Stress in Numbers**
B. Listen and circle the numbers you hear.

1. 13   5. 17
2. 40   6. 80
3. 50   7. 90
4. 16

C. Listen and point to the numbers you hear.

1. It's six-fifteen.
2. It's fifty cents.
3. From 9:30 A.M. to 6:00 P.M.
4. The price is $3.18.

Lesson 7. (page 48)
1. Listening Review
Listen and choose the time you hear.
Use the Answer Sheet.

1.
A: Excuse me. What time is it?
B: It's five o'clock.
A: Okay. Thanks.

2.
A: CTS Drugstore.
B: Yes. When do you open tomorrow?
A: At 8:00.
B: Thanks.
3.
A: When's the next bus?
B: It's at 8:45.
A: Thanks.
4.
A: When's your class today?
B: It's at noon.
A: Are you sure?
B: Yes, of course.

Listen and choose the correct answer.
Use the Answer Sheet.

5. What are your hours on Monday?
6. What time is it?
7. How much is it?
8. When's the party?
9. What day is it?
10. How much is it?

UNIT FOUR
Lesson 1. (page 52)
1. Learn New Words
Look at the pictures. Listen to the words.
Then listen and repeat.

1. January	It's January.
2. February	It's February.
3. March	It's March.
4. April	It's April.
5. May	It's May.
6. June	It's June.
7. July	It's July.
8. August	It's August.
9. September	It's September.
10. October	It's October.
11. November	It's November.
12. December	It's December.
13. cold	It's cold here.
14. warm	It's warm here.
15. hot	It's hot here.
16. rainy	It's rainy here.
17. sunny	It's sunny here.
18. cloudy	It's cloudy here.

Lesson 2. (page 54)
2. Learn New Words
Look at the pictures. Listen to the words.
Then listen and repeat.

1. doctor's appointment	Her doctor's appointment is on May first.
2. computer class	Her computer class is on May third.
3. birthday party	Her birthday party is on May sixth.

4. PTO meeting	Her PTO meeting is on May eighth.
5. job interview	Her job interview is on May ninth.
6. basketball game	Her basketball game is on May eleventh.
7. dentist's appointment	Her dentist's appointment is on May fifteenth.

Lesson 3. (page 56)
1. Learn Ordinal Numbers
Listen to the numbers. Then listen and repeat.

seventeenth	The seventeenth of June is a Sunday.
eighteenth	The eighteenth of June is a Monday.
nineteenth	The nineteenth of June is a Tuesday.
twentieth	The twentieth of June is a Wednesday.
twenty-first	The twenty-first of June is a Thursday.
twenty-second	The twenty-second of June is a Friday.
twenty-third	The twenty-third of June is a Saturday.
twenty-fourth	The twenty-fourth of June is a Sunday.
twenty-fifth	The twenty-fifth of June is a Monday.
twenty-sixth	The twenty-sixth of June is a Tuesday.
twenty-seventh	The twenty-seventh of June is a Wednesday.
twenty-eighth	The twenty-eighth of June is a Thursday.

Lesson 7. (page 64)
1. Listening Review
Listen and choose the word you hear.
Use the Answer Sheet.

1. country	country
2. months	months
3. holidays	holidays
4. family	family
5. dollars	dollars
6. cents	cents
7. state	state
8. cities	cities

Listen and choose the best answer.
Use the Answer Sheet.

9. How many days are in a week?
10. What's the first month of the year?
11. What day is the twenty-first?
12. What day is between Monday and Wednesday?
13. What month is between July and September?
14. When's Thanksgiving in the United States?

Listen and choose the correct appointment card.
Use the Answer Sheet.

15. His appointment is on Wednesday.
16. Her appointment is on Friday.

UNIT FIVE
Lesson 1. (page 68)
1. Learn New Words
Look at the pictures. Listen to the words.
Then listen and repeat.

1. necktie	What is it? It's a necktie.
2. undershirt	What is it? It's an undershirt.
3. briefs	What are they? They're briefs.
4. shoes	What are they? They're shoes.
5. boots	What are they? They're boots.
6. coat	What is it? It's a coat.
7. shirt	What is it? It's a shirt.
8. sweater	What is it? It's a sweater.
9. hat	What is it? It's a hat.
10. T-shirt	What is it? It's a T-shirt.
11. jacket	What is it? It's a jacket.
12. pajamas	What are they? They're pajamas.
13. socks	What are they? They're socks.
14. pants	What are they? They're pants.
15. shorts	What are they? They're shorts.
16. blouse	What is it? It's a blouse.
17. skirt	What is it? It's a skirt.
18. dress	What is it? It's a dress.

Lesson 1. (page 68)
2. Learn New Words
Look at the squares. Listen to the colors.
Then listen and repeat.

1. blue	What color is it? Blue.
2. yellow	What color is it? Yellow.
3. red	What color is it? Red.
4. black	What color is it? Black.
5. brown	What color is it? Brown.
6. green	What color is it? Green.
7. purple	What color is it? Purple.
8. white	What color is it? White.

Lesson 2. (page 70)
1. Learn New Words
Look at the picture. Listen to the words.
Then listen and repeat.

PEOPLE AND PLACES

1. department store	This is Lane's Department Store.
2. fitting room	The fitting room is near the elevator.
3. customer	A customer is near the exit.
4. customer service	There is a woman working at customer service.
5. cashier	The cashier is near the entrance.
6. exit	The exit is across from customer service.
7. entrance	There are people coming in the entrance.

ACTIONS

8. coming into	The man is coming into the sto
9. going into	The woman is going into the elevator.
10. talking	The men are talking about th T-shirt.
11. sleeping	The boy is sleeping near the f ting room.
12. leaving	Marc is leaving the store.
13. running	A cashier is running after To
14. buying	The woman is buying many things.

Lesson 7. (page 112)
1. Listening Review
Look at the family tree. Listen and choose the best answer. Use the Answer Sheet.

1. What's Carol's husband's name?
2. Who's Mei?
3. Who's Ann?
4. Who's Tim's grandmother?

Listen and choose the best answer.
Use the Answer Sheet.

5. Do you live with your parents?
6. What's your brother's name?
7. Does John have children?
8. Who does the dishes in your family?
9. Where do your parents live?
10. What does she do at home?
11. Do you play an instrument?
12. How often do her children cook dinner?

UNIT EIGHT
Lesson 2. (page 118)
2. Learn New Words
Look at the picture. Listen to the words.
Then listen and repeat.

1. headache	Tina has a headache.
2. earache	Martin's son has an earache.
3. fever	Louis has a fever.
4. runny nose	Ken has a runny nose.
5. cough	Rose's daughter has a cough.
6. sore throat	Donna has a sore throat.
7. backache	Erik has a backache.
8. stomachache	Tom has a stomachache.

Lesson 3. (page 120)
1. Learn New Words
Look at the pictures. Listen to the words.
Then listen and repeat.

1. A: Drink liquids. B: Drink what? A: Liquids.
2. A: Eat soft foods. B: Eat what? A: Soft foods.
3. A: Take cough medicine. B: Take what? A: Cough medicine.
4. A: Take aspirin. B: Take what? A: Aspirin.
5. A: Use ear drops. B: Use what? A: Ear drops.
6. A: Rest. B: Rest? A: Rest.
7. A: Put heat on it. B: Put what on it? A: Heat.
8. A: Put ice on it. B: Put what on it? A: Ice.
9. A: Bandage it. B: Do what to it? A: Bandage it.
10. A: Keep it dry. B: Keep it what? A: Dry.

Lesson 5. (page 124)
1. Learn New Words
Look at the pictures below. Listen to the words.
Then listen and repeat.

1. He is choking. What's the matter? He's choking.
2. He is bleeding. What's the matter? He's bleeding.
3. She is having a heart attack. What's the matter? She's having a heart attack.
4. She isn't breathing. What's the matter? She isn't breathing.

Lesson 5. (page 125)
Window on Pronunciation
Linking Vowel to Vowel with a *Y* or *W* Sound
Listen and complete the conversations.

1.
   A: This is 911.
   B: My mother is hurt. She's choking.
   A: Where are you?
   B: I'm at 414 Pine Street.
2.
   A: Where are you?
   B: We're at home.
   A: How's Paul?
   B: He's resting.

Lesson 6. (page 126)
1. Learn New Words
Look at the pictures. Listen to the words.
Then listen and repeat.

1. Main Entrance	Where's the main entrance?
2. Emergency Entrance	Where's the emergency entrance?
3. Lobby	Where's the lobby?
4. Visitors' Lounge	Where's the visitors' lounge?

Lesson 7. (page 128)
1. Listening Review
Listen to the conversations. Choose the problem you hear. Use the Answer Sheet.

1.
   A: What's the matter?
   B: My wrist hurts.
   A: Can you move it?
   B: Yes, a little.
2.
   A: What's the matter with Thomas?
   B: He has a really bad headache.
   A: That's too bad.
3.
   A: Can I help you?
   B: Yes, I have an appointment with Dr. Jones.
   A: What are you here for, Mr. Munro?
   B: It's my ear. I have an earache.
4.
   A: Hi, I'm Dr. Coffin.
   B: Hi, Dr. Coffin. I'm John Fernandez.
   A: Nice to meet you. So what's the problem?
   B: Oh, I have a sore shoulder.

Listen and choose the best answer.
Use the Answer Sheet.

5. What should I do for my backache?
6. What should you do for a stomachache?
7. What number should you call for an ambulance?
8. Should you call 911 for a sore toe?

UNIT NINE
Lesson 1. (page 132)
1. Learn New Words
Look at the pictures. Listen to the words.
Then listen and repeat.

1. sofa	Where's the sofa?
2. bookcase	Where's the bookcase?
3. lamp	Where's the lamp?
4. smoke alarm	Where's the smoke alarm?
5. carpet	Where's the carpet?
6. mirror	Where's the mirror?
7. sink	Where's the sink?
8. shower	Where's the shower?
9. toilet	Where's the toilet?
10. bathtub	Where's the bathtub?
11. drawer	Where's the drawer?
12. cabinet	Where's the cabinet?
13. closet	Where's the closet?
14. refrigerator	Where's the refrigerator?
15. stove	Where's the stove?
16. dresser	Where's the dresser?
17. bed	Where's the bed?

Lesson 2. (page 134)
1. Learn New Words
Look at the pictures. Listen to the words.
Then listen and repeat.

1. pool	Does your house have a pool?
2. patio	Does your house have a patio?
3. front yard	Does your house have a front yard?
4. carport	Does your house have a carport?
5. driveway	Does your house have a driveway?
6. garage	Does your house have a garage?
7. porch	Does your house have a porch?
8. backyard	Does your house have a backyard?
9. garden	Does your house have a garden?

Lesson 3. (page 136)
1. Learn New Words
Look at the pictures. Listen to the words.
Then listen and repeat.

1. fell down the stairs
   A: What happened to Joe?
   B: He fell down the stairs.
2. fell off a ladder
   A: What happened to Sylvia?
   B: She fell off a ladder.
3. fell off a chair
   A: What happened to Carol?
   B: She fell off a chair.
4. slipped in the shower
   A: What happened to Mike?
   B: He slipped in the shower.
5. cut his hand with a knife
   A: What happened to Nick?
   B: He cut his hand with a knife.
6. tripped on the carpet
   A: What happened to Donna?
   B: She tripped on the carpet.

Lesson 4. (page 138)
1. Learn New Words
Look at the pictures. Listen to the words.
Then listen and repeat.

1. apartment	Do you live in an apartment?
2. condo	Do you live in a condo?
3. mobile home	Do you live in a mobile home?

Lesson 4. (page 138)
2. Write
Read and listen to the classified ads.
Find and write the abbreviations for these words.

a. House for rent. Three bedrooms, two bathrooms. Near schools. Patio and pool. $1350 per month. Call Eileen at 555-4000.
b. For rent. Mobile home. One bedroom, one bathroom. Near public pool. $795 per month. Call Joe, 555-1928.
c. House for sale. Three bedrooms, two bathrooms, big kitchen, two fireplaces, patio, garage. $210,000. Call Marlene, 555-1200, ext. 15.
d. For rent, two bedroom, two bathroom apartment. Pool and patio. $950. Call John, 555-4583.
e. For sale. Two bedroom, one-and-a-half bathroom condo. Near stores. $175,000. Call Smith Realty, 555-6767.
f. Apartment for rent. One bedroom, one bathroom. $825 per month. Call 555-9904.
g. Condo for rent. Two bedrooms, one bathroom, garage, near schools, $1100 per month. Call Bev, 555-4954.
h. Mobile home for rent. Two bedroom, one bathroom, patio, no pets, $875 per month. Call 555-9948.

Lesson 6. (page 142)
1. Learn New Words
Look at the bills below. Listen to the words.
Then listen and repeat.

1. account number	The account number is 6464560483-0.
2. amount due	The amount due is $133.19.
3. amount enclosed	The amount enclosed is $133.19.
4. new charges	The amount of new charges is $56.29.

Lesson 7. (page 144)
1. Listening Review
Listen to the conversations. Choose the correct picture.
Use the Answer Sheet.

1. A: Where's my blue sweater?
   B: It's in your dresser.
   A: Oh, thanks.
2. A: Where's Joe?
   B: He's in the kitchen
   A: What's he doing there?
   B: He's cleaning the stove.
3. A: I'm calling about the apartment for rent.
   B: Yes. What do you want to know?
   A: Can you tell me, does it have a patio?
   B: Yes, it does. It has a beautiful patio.
4. A: What happened to your brother?
   B: He fell off a ladder.
   A: That's too bad. Is he okay now?
   B: Yes, he's fine.

Listen and choose the best answer.
Use the Answer Sheet.

5. Where's the smoke alarm?
6. Does the apartment have a shower?
7. Do you live in an apartment?
8. How many bedrooms does it have?

UNIT TEN
Lesson 1. (page 148)
1. Learn New Words
Look at the pictures. Listen to the words.
Then listen and repeat.

1. chef — A chef cooks food.
2. office manager — An office manager uses a computer.
3. plumber — A plumber repairs sinks and toilets.
4. stylist — A stylist cuts hair.
5. child care worker — A child care worker takes care of children.
6. mechanic — A mechanic fixes cars.
7. mover — A mover lifts heavy things.
8. construction worker — A construction worker builds things.
9. truck driver — A truck driver drives a truck.
10. landscaper — A landscaper takes care of plants.

Lesson 3. (page 152)
2. Listen and Take Notes
Listen to Rosa's job interview. Write the missing information.

Interviewer: So, Rosa, tell me about yourself.
Interviewee: Well, I'm really interested in retail. Right now I'm the store manager at Lane's. I got the job in 2000.
Interviewer: That's very interesting. Do you like your job?
Interviewee: Yes, very much. I'm really sad Lane's is closing soon.
Interviewer: Yes, that is too bad. And what did you do before that?
Interviewee: Well, I was a salesclerk at Lane's for almost two years, from 1998 to 2000. Then I got promoted to store manager.
Interviewer: Yes, I see.
Interviewee: And before that, I worked as a salesclerk at a store called The Elephant's Trunk.
Interviewer: When was that?
Interviewee: I worked there from 1996 to 1998. I learned a lot there.

Lesson 7. (page 160)
1. Listening Review
Listen and choose the correct answer.
Use the Answer Sheet.

1. What do stylists do?
2. Can he lift heavy things?
3. Did she work last week?
4. Is it a part-time job?
5. Why did you leave your last job?
6. Why should I hire you?
7. Sam worked 10 hours last week. He earns $20 an hour. How much did he earn last week?
8. Mei worked 40 hours last week. She earns $20 an hour. How much did she earn last week?

Lesson 7. (page 160)
2. Dictation
Listen and write the questions you hear.

1. Did you work last year?
2. Can you drive a car?
3. Do you have a job now?

Numbers in parentheses indicate unit numbers.

accident (9)
account number (9)
across from (2)
address (1)
after (3)
afternoon (3)
aisle (6)
always (6)
A.M. (3)
ambulance (2)
amount (3)
amount due (9)
amount enclosed (9)
ankle (8)
apartment (9)
apple (6)
appointment (4)
April (4)
area code (1)
arm (8)
ask (1)
ask questions (10)
aspirin (8)
ATM (2)
audiobook (2)
August (4)
aunt (7)
back (8)
backache (8)
backyard (9)
bag (6)
bakery (6)
banana (6)
bandage (8)
bank (2)
basketball game (4)
bathroom (9)
bathtub (9)
be (1)
be late (10)
bean (6)
bed (9)
bedroom (9)
before (3)
benefits (10)
between (2)
big (5)
birthday party (4)
birthplace (1)
black (5)
bleed (8)
blouse (5)
blue (5)
board (1)
book (1)
bookcase (9)
bookmobile (2)
boot (5)
bottle (6)
box (6)
bread (6)
breathe (8)
briefs (5)

brother (7)
brown (5)
budget (7)
build (10)
bus (2)
bus driver (1)
bus stop (2)
butter (6)
buy (5)
cabinet (9)
calendar (1)
can (6)
cap (5)
capital (2)
car (2)
carefully (10)
carpet (9)
carport (9)
carrot (6)
carton (6)
cashier (1)
cents (3)
cereal (6)
chair (1)
cheap (6)
check (3)
check number (3)
checkout counter (6)
checkout desk (2)
cheese (6)
chef (10)
chest (8)
chew gum (10)
chicken (6)
child care (7)
child care worker (10)
children (7)
children's book (2)
choke (8)
circle (1)
city (1)
clean (6)
clock (1)
close (1)
closed (3)
closet (9)
clothing (7)
cloudy (4)
coat (5)
cold (4)
coming into (5)
comma (1)
community center (2)
computer (1)
condo (9)
construction worker (10)
cook (10)
cook dinner (7)
cooked (6)
cough (8)
cough medicine (8)
country (1)
coupon (6)

crosswalk (2)
cup (6)
customer (5)
customer service (5)
cut (5)
dairy (6)
dance (7)
daughter (7)
day (3)
December (4)
delicious (6)
dentist (1)
department store (5)
desk (1)
dime (3)
dining room (9)
dish (7)
divided by (5)
divorced (1)
doctor (1)
dollar (3)
door (1)
do the laundry (7)
drawer (9)
dress (5/noun)
dress (10/verb)
dresser (9)
drink (8)
drive (10)
driveway (9)
drugstore (2)
dry (8)
ear (8)
earache (8)
ear drops (8)
east (2)
eat (6)
education (7)
egg (6)
eight (1)
eighteen (3)
eighteenth (4)
eighth (4)
eighty (3)
elbow (8)
eleven (1)
eleventh (4)
emergency entrance (8)
enter (2)
entrance (5)
equals (2)
evening (3)
exit (5)
expense (7)
expensive (6)
extra large (5)
eye (8)
fall (9)
father (7)
February (4)
feet (8)
female (1)
fever (8)

fifteen (3)
fifteenth (4)
fifth (4)
fifty (3)
fine (1)
finger (8)
fire station (2)
first (4)
fish (6)
fitting room (5)
five (1)
fix (7)
flammable (8)
floor (1)
food (6)
foot (8)
forty (3)
four (1)
fourteen (3)
fourteenth (4)
fourth (4)
Friday (3)
front yard (9)
frozen foods (6)
fruit (6)
gallon (8)
garage (9)
garden (9)
gas station (2)
gender (1)
gift (7)
go to (1)
going into (5)
grain (6)
granddaughter (7)
grandfather (7)
grandmother (7)
grandson (7)
grape (6)
green (5)
grocery (7)
half-dollar (3)
hand (8)
hat (5)
have (6)
head (8)
headache (8)
heart attack (8)
heat (8)
heavy (10)
hole (5)
honey (6)
hospital (2)
hot (4)
hours (3)
husband (7)
ice (6)
indoor (10)
in back of (2)
in front of (2)
internally (8)
jacket (5)
January (4)

jar (6)
job interview (4)
juice (6)
July (4)
June (4)
kitchen (9)
knee (8)
knife (9)
ladder (9)
lamp (9)
landscaper (10)
large (5)
late (10)
laundromat (2)
leave (5)
left (2)
leg (8)
less than (2)
lettuce (6)
librarian (2)
library (2)
library card (2)
lift (10)
like (6)
liquid (8)
listen (1)
listen carefully (10)
listen to music (7)
living room (9)
loaf (6)
lobby (8)
long (5)
look at (6)
look for (5)
loose (5)
machinist (1)
magazine (2)
mailbox (2)
main entrance (8)
make (10)
make the bed (7)
male (1)
map (1)
March (4)
marital status (1)
married (1)
May (4)
meat (6)
mechanic (10)
medium (5)
men (5)
middle name (1)
midnight (3)
milk (6)
minus (2)
minute (3)
mirror (9)
mobile home (9)
Monday (3)
month (4)
mop (6)
more than (2)
morning (3)

mother (7)
mouth (8)
mover (10)
movie theater (2)
Mr. (1)
Mrs. (1)
Ms. (1)
near (2)
neatly (10)
neck (8)
necktie (5)
never (6)
new charges (9)
newspaper (7)
next to (2)
nickel (3)
night (3)
nine (1)
nineteen (3)
nineteenth (4)
ninety (3)
ninth (4)
noodles (6)
noon (3)
north (2)
nose (8)
notebook (1)
November (4)
nurse (1)
nut (6)
occupation (1)
o'clock (3)
October (4)
office manager (10)
oil (6)
on sale (6)
on the corner of (2)
one (1)
one way (2)
onion (6)
open (1/verb)
open (3/adj.)
orange (6)
ounce (6)
outdoor (10)
out of reach (8)
package (6)
pajamas (5)
pants (5)
parent (7)
park (2)
parking lot (2)
partner (1)
patio (9)
pay phone (2)
pay the bills (7)
peanut (6)
pen (1)
pencil (1)
penny (3)
people (1)
period (1)
personal check (3)

pharmacist (1)
piece of paper (1)
pint (8)
play an instrument (7)
play cards (7)
play soccer (7)
plumber (10)
plus (2)
P.M. (3)
poison (8)
police officer (1)
police station (2)
pool (9)
porch (9)
post office (2)
pound (6)
practice (1)
pregnant (8)
price (5)
price tag (5)
produce section (6)
PTO meeting (4)
purple (5)
push a cart (6)
quart (8)
quarter (3)
question mark (1)
question (10)
rainy (4)
raise (1)
raw (6)
read (1)
receipt (5)
red (5)
refrigerator (9)
reliable (10)
rent (7)
repair (10)
repeat (1)
rest (8)
restaurant (2)
restroom (6)
rice (6)
right (2)
run (5)
runny nose (8)
sale (9)
salesclerk (1)
Saturday (3)
savings (7)
say (1)
school (2)
scissors (5)
second (4)
September (4)
serving (6)
seven (1)
seventeen (3)
seventeenth (4)
seventh (4)
seventy (3)
shake hands (10)

shirt (5)
shoe (5)
shopping cart (6)
short (5)
shorts (5)
shoulder (8)
shower (9)
shrimp (6)
sidewalk (2)
signature (3)
single (1)
sink (9)
sister (7)
sit down (1)
six (1)
sixteen (3)
sixteenth (4)
sixth (4)
sixty (3)
size (5)
skirt (5)
slice (6)
sleep (5)
slip (9)
small (5)
smoke alarm (9)
smoking (3)
sock (5)
sofa (9)
soft food (8)
sometimes (6)
son (7)
sore (8)
south (2)
stairs (9)
stand in line (6)
stand up (1)
state (1)
stomach (8)
stomachache (8)
stop (2)
stoplight (2)
stove (9)
street (1)
student (1)
stylist (10)
sugar (6)
Sunday (3)
sunny (4)
supermarket (2)
sweater (5)
table (1)
tailor (5)
take care of (10)
take out (1)
take pictures (7)
talk to (5)
taxi (2)
teacher (1)
telephone number (1)
tell stories (7)
ten (1)

tenth (4)
terrible (6)
third (4)
thirteen (3)
thirteenth (4)
thirtieth (4)
thirty (3)
thirty-five (3)
thirty-one (3)
three (1)
throat (8)
Thursday (3)
tight (5)
times (5)
toe (8)
toilet (9)
tomato (6)
too (5)
transportation (7)
trash (7)
trip (9)
truck (2)
truck driver (10)
T-shirt (5)
Tuesday (3)
turn (2)
twelfth (4)
twelve (3)
twentieth (4)
twenty (3)
twenty-one (3)
two (1)
uncle (7)
undershirt (5)
usually (6)
utilities (7)
vegetable (6)
video (2)
visitor's lounge (8)
wall (1)
warm (4)
wash (7)
weather (4)
wear (5)
Wednesday (3)
week (3)
west (2)
white (5)
wife (7)
window (1)
women (5)
wrist (8)
write (1)
yellow (5)
yogurt (6)
zero (1)
zip code (1)

ACADEMIC SKILLS

Grammar
Adverbs, 91, 96, 102–103
and as coordinating conjunction, 99
Capital letters, 67
Contractions, 18
Nouns, singular and plural, 59
Paragraph indentation, 131
Possessive adjectives, 19
Possessive nouns, 14, 19
Prepositions of location, 22
Pronouns
    Object, 75
    Subject, 18
Punctuation, 11, 35
Questions
    Information questions with *be*, 51,
      70, 81
    Information questions with simple
      present (*do*), 101, 104, 112
    Information questions with simple
      past, 147
    Yes/No questions with *be*, 37, 50–51
    Yes/No questions with simple
      present, 101
    Yes/No questions with simple past,
      149
    with *do you like*, 85
    with *how many*, 53
    with *how much*, 41, 47
    with *is there, are there*, 23
    There is/There are, 21, 24
Verbs
    can for ability, 117
    does and *doesn't*, 107
    Future tense with *be going to*, 155
    Irregular verbs (past tense), 133, 137,
      146–147
    Present continuous tense, 69, 82–83
    should and *shouldn't* for advice, 121
    Simple past tense, 133, 137, 139
    Simple present tense, 103, 104,
      114–115
    Simple present with *be*, 5, 18

Listening
Advertisements, 96
Alphabet, 2
Comprehension, 16, 32, 48, 64, 74, 80, 96,
    112, 128, 144, 152, 160
Conversations, 2–3, 4, 12–13, 20, 22, 24,
    26, 28–29, 36, 38, 40, 44–45, 54, 56,
    60–61, 70, 72, 76–77, 86, 88, 92–93,
    114–115, 116, 118, 120, 124–125,
    128, 136, 140–141, 147, 150, 156–157

Dates, 64
Instructions, 8–9 (classroom)
Introductions, 2–3, 12
Names, 2–3
Numbers, 36, 45, 54, 56
Personal information, 4, 10
Questions, 4, 33, 49, 80, 160
Statements, 74
Telephone, 44–45, 60–61, 108–109,
    124–125, 140–141
Time, 36-37, 48
Vocabulary, 6, 10, 14, 16, 20, 22, 24, 26,
    30, 36, 38, 40, 42, 52–53, 54, 56, 64,
    68, 70, 72, 76, 84, 86, 88, 96, 100, 102,
    104, 110, 112, 116, 118, 120, 122,
    124, 126, 132, 134, 136, 138, 142, 148

Math
Addition and subtraction, 43, 90
Dates, 57
Multiplication and division, 73, 95, 111,
    123
Numbers, 9, 27, 36, 54–57, 64, 70
Symbols, 27
Weights and measures, 88–89, 90–91,
    123
Word problems, 151

Pronunciation
Intonation in *yes/no* questions, 93
Linking consonant to vowel, 109
Linking vowel to vowel with *y* or *w*
    sounds, 125
Long vowel sounds *i* and *e,* 13
Short *a* and long *a,* 61
Stress in compound nouns, 141
Stressing important words in sentences,
    157
Syllable stress in numbers, 45
th sounds, 29
Vowel sounds in *shoes* and *should,* 77

Reading
Abbreviations, 138–139
Advertisements, 14–15, 90–91, 138–139,
    150–151
Applications, 10–11, 158–159
Appointment cards, 56–57, 64–65
Bills, 142–143
Calendars, 62–63
Checks, 42–43, 142–143
Comprehension, 46–47, 79, 90–91,
    94–95, 98, 122–123, 130, 136–137,
    138–139, 142–143, 150–151,
    154–155, 158
Dates, 56–57, 64–65

Description, 26, 34, 106–107
Directories, 70
Graphs, charts, and maps, 22, 26–27, 42,
    49, 84–85, 94–95, 127, 130, 136–137
Instructions, 8–9 (classroom), 98–99
Labels on medications, 122–133
Library cards, 30–31
Math symbols, 27
Memos, 79
Questions, 26, 30–31, 53, 83
Receipts, 72–73
Recipes, 98
Schedules, 62–63 (academic)
Signs, 24–25, 38–39, 46–47, 70–71
Statements, 18, 26, 30–31, 34, 58–59
Stories, 18, 34–35, 66–67, 74–75, 162
Telephone books, 20
Time, 36, 48
Vocabulary, 10, 15

Speaking
Conversations, 2–3, 4, 12–13, 17, 20, 22,
    24, 26, 28–29, 33, 36, 38, 40, 44–45,
    49, 54, 56, 60–61, 65, 70, 72, 76–77,
    81, 86, 88, 92–93, 97, 113, 114–115,
    116, 118, 120, 124–125, 128–129,
    136, 140–141, 145, 147, 150,
    156–157, 161
Describing people, 78, 104
Describing things, 76–77, 86–87
Giving directions, 22–23
Instructions, 8–9 (classroom)
Introductions, 2–3, 12–13
Math symbols, 9, 27
Opinions, 78, 84, 110, 131
Personal information, 4, 10
Questions
    Answering, 6, 14, 26, 28–29, 33, 37,
      41, 49, 68, 70, 78, 102, 117, 120,
      148–149
    Asking, 6, 14, 26, 28–29, 33, 37, 41,
      49, 53, 56, 58, 68, 70, 72, 78, 85,
      88, 100, 102, 104, 117, 118, 120,
      129, 131, 147, 148–149, 159
Statements, 43, 74–75, 78, 86, 94, 104,
    110–111, 118–119, 120, 126, 134, 154
Telephone, 44–45, 60–61, 108–109,
    124–125, 140-141

Writing
Advertisements, 138, 150
Applications, 10–11, 31, 158–159
Appointment cards, 64
Calendars, 62–63
Checks, 42, 143

Conversations, 114
Dates, 55, 56-57
Description, 76, 106, 134, 148
Dictation, 32, 80, 96, 160
Graphs, charts, and maps, 3, 4, 8, 15, 17,
    35, 42, 47, 49, 52, 56, 58–59, 63, 68,
    84, 85, 88, 94–95, 97, 100, 106, 111,
    113, 116, 131, 134, 150, 152
Instructions, 8, 99
Lists, 20, 52, 72, 84, 90, 111, 122, 163
Money, 40-41
Name tags, 3
Numbers, 42
Opinions, 152
Paragraphs, 102, 131 (expository)
Personal information, 3, 17, 18–19
Questions, 50–51, 83, 101, 104, 114–115
Questions, answering, 50, 62, 111
Receipts, 72
Recipes, 99
Statements, 4, 18–19, 38, 46, 52, 74, 76,
    79, 82, 86, 95, 102, 104, 106, 114,
    118, 126, 132, 134, 146, 148, 150,
    152–153, 154
Stories, 34-35, 67, 152, 162
Time, 36-38, 45
Vocabulary, 6, 10, 15, 30, 36-37, 38,
    40–41, 52–53, 66, 68, 100, 102–103,
    132

APPLICATION

Community, 30–31, 46–47, 126–127
Family, 62–63, 94–95, 110–111, 142–143
Work, 14–15, 78–79, 158–159

LEARNER LOGS

17, 33, 49, 65, 81, 97, 113, 129, 145, 161

LIFE SKILLS

Consumer Education

Advertisements, 90–91, 96, 138–139
Checks, 42-43
Clothing items, 68–69, 72–73, 74–75,
    76–77, 78–79, 80–81
Counting money, 40–41
Food items, 84–89, 92–97
Hours of operation, 46
Household/housing, 110–111, 132--145
Making transactions, 77, 81, 92–93
Prices, 41, 47, 72–73, 80–81, 90–91,
    92–93, 96–97
Product labels, 122–123
Receipts, 72–73, 90
Sales, 72–73, 93

Shopping lists, 90
Sizes, 72–73
Stores, 20–21, 70–71
Utility companies, 142

Environment and World

Building maps, 126–127
City maps, 22–25, 32–33
United States map, 26–27
Weather, 52–53, 65
World map, 4-5

Family and Parenting

Family members, 100–113
Family responsibilities, 102–103
Household/housing, 110–111, 132–145
Recipes, 98–99

Government and Community

Agencies, 20
Leisure activities, 104–105
Library, 22, 30–31
Medical services, 124–125, 126–127
Places in the community, 20–25, 32–33
Post Office, 20, 22–23, 24–25
Public services, 20, 22, 24–25
Signs, 24–25, 38–39, 46-47, 70–71

Group Work

3, 4, 88, 120, 148

Resources

Community places, 20–25, 32–33
Library, 22, 30–31
Post Office, 20, 22–23, 24–25
Public services, 20, 22, 24–25

Health and Nutrition

Accidents, 136–137
Body part identification, 116–117
Foods and food groups, 84–85, 88–89,
    94–99
Health care vocabulary, 118–129
Hospital, 126-127
Medical advice, 120, 128–129
Medicine labels and use, 122–123
Symptoms and illnesses, 116–117,
    118–119, 120–121, 124–125,
    128–129

Interpersonal Communication

Introductions, greetings, and farewells,
    2–5, 12–13
Personal information, 4–5, 10–11, 17, 50
Understanding instructions, 8–9, 98–99

Learning to Learn

Problem solving skills, 74–75
Thinking skills, 74–75, 90, 122–123

Pair Work

2–3, 6, 8–9, 10, 12–13, 14, 22–23, 24,
28--29, 36–37, 38, 40–41, 43, 44, 51,
52--53, 56, 60–61, 68, 70, 72, 76–77, 78,
83, 84, 88, 92–93, 97, 100–101, 102, 104,
106, 108–109, 110–111, 113, 114, 116,
118, 120, 124–125, 126, 129, 134, 136,
140–141, 145, 147, 150, 156-157, 159,
161

Safety and Security

Emergency procedures, 124–125, 128
Product labels, 122–123
Warning labels and symbols, 122–123

Telephone Communication

Answering, 108
Making a call, 108
Making appointments, 60–61, 65
Messages, taking and leaving, 109
Obtaining information, 44–45, 140–141
911 use, 124–125

Time and Money

Appointments, 60–61, 64–65
Bills, 142–143
Budgets, 110–111, 113
Days of the week, 38–39
Calendar, 54–55, 62–63
Checks, 42–43, 142–143
Clock time, 36–39, 48–49
Coins and currency, 40–41
Date format, 56–57
Months, 52–53, 64–65
Numbers, cardinal and ordinal, 9, 27, 36,
    54–57, 64, 70
Receipts, 72–73

Transportation and Travel

Geographical directions and locations,
    26–27
Traffic signs, 24–25
Types, 24–25

TOPICS

Activities, 102–105
Body Parts, 116–117
Classroom, 6–7, 8–9, 16
Clothing, 68–69, 72–81
Colors, 68–69
Community, 22–25, 28–33

Map of the United States

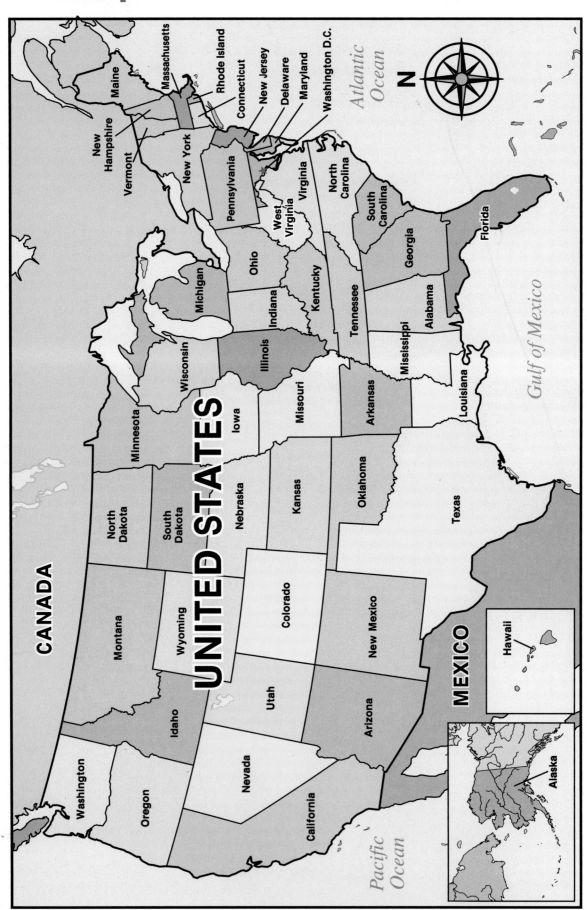